The Hound *Baskerville*

SIR ARTHUR CONAN DOYLE

Level 5

Retold by Alan Ronaldson
Series Editors: Andy Hopkins and Jocelyn Potter

04037680

Pearson Education Limited
Edinburgh Gate, Harlow,
Essex CM20 2JE, England
and Associated Companies throughout the world.

ISBN: 978-1-4058-6248-6

First published in the Longman Simplified English Series 1976
This adaptation first published by Addison Wesley Longman Limited
in the Longman Fiction Series 1996
First published by Penguin Books 1999

5 7 9 10 8 6

Original copyright © The Copyright holders of the Sir Arthur Conan Doyle
works, reproduced by kind permission of Jonathan Clowes Ltd London,
on behalf of Andrea Plunket & Administrator
Text copyright © Penguin Books Ltd 1999
This edition copyright © Pearson Education Ltd 2008

Typeset by Graphicraft Ltd, Hong Kong
Set in 11/14pt Bembo
Printed in China
SWTC/05

Published by Pearson Education Ltd in association with
Penguin Books Ltd, both companies being subsidiaries of Pearson Plc

For a complete list of the titles available in the Penguin Readers series please write to your local
Pearson Longman office or to: Penguin Readers Marketing Department, Pearson Education,
Edinburgh Gate, Harlow, Essex CM20 2JE, England.

Contents

Introduction

'Footprints?'

'Footprints.'

'A man's or woman's?'

*Dr Mortimer looked strangely at us for a minute, and his voice sank
almost to a whisper as he answered:*

'Mr Holmes, they were the footprints of a gigantic hound!'

One day, Sherlock Holmes, the great detective, and his friend and
colleague Dr Watson receive a visit from Dr Mortimer, who lives
in a small village on Dartmoor, a large area of wild moorland in
south-west England. They listen to his strange story about the
death of his dear friend and neighbour, Sir Charles Baskerville,
and of the terrible curse of the evil hound that has terrorized the
Baskerville family for more than two hundred years. Holmes is
interested in the story and sends Watson to Baskerville Hall, on
Dartmoor, to find out more. Watson soon comes into contact
with a series of mysterious people: Selden, an escaped prisoner;
Stapleton, a strange naturalist who lives with his beautiful sister;
the servant Barrymore and his wife. All behave suspiciously, and
all have dark secrets. It soon becomes clear that the newly arrived
young Sir Henry Baskerville, who has been left the hall by his
uncle, Sir Charles Baskerville, is in terrible danger. Will Watson
be able to protect him? Where is Sherlock Holmes? Has he really
left Sir Henry to face the family curse alone? And what is that
frightening, unearthly sound that sweeps across the moors? Is it
just the sound of the wind, or can it really be the wild cry of a
ghostly hound?

Before he became a writer, Conan Doyle studied medicine, and
much of the character of Sherlock Holmes is taken from one of

his teachers, Joseph Bell. When patients came to see him, Bell was often able to give them information about their jobs, habits and even their illnesses before they had said a word. He taught his students the importance of small details, which is one of the skills needed by all great detectives. Sherlock Holmes is more interested in the activities of the brain and the use of faultless logic than in the imperfections of often illogical human emotion. He shows no interest in women and his only friend is Dr Watson, which makes him seem at times more like a machine than a human being.

The reading public, however, were not interested in Holmes's less attractive qualities. After two Sherlock Holmes novels, *A Study in Scarlet* (1888) and *The Sign of Four* (1890), short stories about the detective began to appear regularly in the *Strand* magazine, and Holmes quickly became a national hero. The magazine sold more copies than it had ever done before. Much of the stories' success was due to Sidney Paget's wonderful drawings of the great detective, which show him in his famous hat and smoking his pipe – details which rarely appear in the stories themselves.

Despite the success of Sherlock Holmes, however, Conan Doyle dreamt of becoming a more 'serious' writer and of writing different types of books. After he had agreed to write a second series of stories for the *Strand*, therefore, he decided that his detective had to die. The last story in this second series, 'The Final Problem' (December 1893), ends with Holmes in Switzerland, fighting for his life with his greatest enemy, Moriarty. When Watson arrives, both men have disappeared. They have, it seems, both fallen to their deaths. The public were shocked and angry, unable to believe that their hero was dead. Conan Doyle himself was surprised by this reaction, but refused for several years to write another Sherlock Holmes story. In 1901, however, he changed his mind.

In March of that year, he was on holiday with his friend

Bertram Fletcher Robinson, who told him about his childhood in Devon, in south-west England. Conan Doyle was particularly interested in stories that his friend had heard of ghostly hounds that wandered over Dartmoor, and thought that this would make a good starting point for a novel. However, he needed a strong central character. He eventually decided that, instead of creating a new character, he would make it another Sherlock Holmes story. He was unwilling to bring Sherlock Holmes back to life, so he decided to write a story that happened before Holmes's 'death' in Switzerland. Of course, Conan Doyle's decision to write another Sherlock Holmes story was probably coloured by financial considerations and the knowledge that the public would go wild with excitement about the return of their hero!

Later that month, Robinson took Conan Doyle on a tour of Dartmoor and the idea for *The Hound of the Baskervilles* began to take shape. Interestingly, Robinson had a driver called Harry Baskerville, which explains how Conan Doyle chose the book's title. Later, the author gave the driver a signed copy of the book with this message inside: 'To Harry Baskerville, with apologies for using the name.' When *The Hound of the Baskervilles* first appeared in the *Strand* in August 1901, the magazine immediately sold 30,000 more copies than usual.

Two years after the great success of *The Hound of the Baskervilles*, Conan Doyle really did bring Sherlock Holmes back to life. In 1903, an American company offered him the enormous sum of 25,000 dollars for six stories, and he could not refuse. In the short story 'The Empty House', Holmes returns to Baker Street – to the great shock of Dr Watson! It seemed that only Moriarty had died in Switzerland. Holmes had spent the next two years travelling because other enemies had also wanted to kill him. This did not make much sense, but readers did not care. Their hero had returned, and nothing else mattered. After his third series of adventures, *The Return of Sherlock Holmes* (1904), there was one final novel, *The Valley of Fear* (1915) and two more collections of short stories, *His Last Bow* (1917) and *The Casebook of Sherlock Holmes* (1927).

In total, Conan Doyle wrote four Sherlock Holmes novels and fifty-six short stories. However, as we have already seen, he did not want to be remembered only as the creator of Sherlock Holmes. He wrote books of historical fiction, including *The Exploits of Brigadier Gerard* (1896) and *The Adventures of Gerard* (1896). He also wrote science fiction stories, the most famous of which is *The Lost World* (1912). His desire to escape the enormous success of Sherlock Holmes is perhaps understandable, but without Sherlock Holmes he would almost certainly not be remembered today.

Sherlock Holmes is the most famous fictional detective in the world, and is probably the best-known character in literature. There have been hundreds of films about his stories, and many actors have become famous for playing the part of Sherlock Holmes. Perhaps one of the best was Basil Rathbone, who made fourteen Sherlock Holmes films for Hollywood between 1939 and 1946.

Arthur Conan Doyle was one of ten children born into an Irish family in Edinburgh in 1859. His father, Charles Doyle, was an artist, but he drank too much and life was hard for the Doyle family. Young Arthur was sent away to a Catholic school in the north of England, and rarely saw his father.

From 1876 to 1881, Conan Doyle studied medicine at the University of Edinburgh, then worked as a ship's doctor on a journey to the West African coast. In 1882, he started work as a doctor in Plymouth, but without much success. As his medical work did not keep him busy enough, he amused himself by writing stories, the first of which appeared in *Chambers's Edinburgh Journal* before he was twenty.

After a move to Southsea, he began to write more. His first important work, *A Study in Scarlet*, appeared in *Beeton's Christmas Annual* for 1887 and introduced the reading public for the first time to Sherlock Holmes. Rudyard Kipling, the famous English writer, congratulated Conan Doyle on his book.

In 1885, Conan Doyle married Louisa Hawkins, who died in 1906. A year after his wife's death, he married Jean Leckie, whom he had met and fallen in love with in 1897. Conan Doyle had five children – two with his first wife and three with his second.

In 1891, he moved to London and, after a short time as an unsuccessful eye doctor, gave up all medical work to become a full-time writer. Apart from his Sherlock Holmes stories and other fiction, he wrote a book about the war between the British and the Dutch in South Africa, *The Great Boer War* (1900). He always believed that the king made him 'Sir' Arthur Conan Doyle as a reward for this book, which defended British action in South Africa at the time.

Conan Doyle tried twice, without success, to become a member of the British parliament. He became a strong believer in equality for all under the law, and helped to free two men who had been wrongly sent to prison. One of them, a lawyer called George Edalji, had been unjustly imprisoned for harming animals. After Edalji had been freed with Conan Doyle's help, important changes were made to British law to make it more difficult for innocent people to be sent to prison. This story is told in Julian Barnes's 2005 novel, *Arthur and George*.

After the deaths of his son, his brother and his two nephews in World War I, Conan Doyle became interested in the spiritual world and the search for scientific proof of life after death. He died in 1930, aged seventy-one. He had done many interesting things in his life but, like Moriarty, had been unable to kill Sherlock Holmes. Even today, people write to Holmes's Baker Street address (now a bank), asking for the detective's help and advice. Sherlock Holmes never really existed, but he always refused to die. To his readers, he is still alive today – the greatest detective that the world has ever known.

Chapter 1   Dr Mortimer's Visit

Mr Sherlock Holmes, who was usually very late in the mornings, except on those quite frequent occasions when he did not go to bed all night, was sitting at the breakfast table. I was standing in front of the fire, and I picked up the walking stick which our visitor had left behind the night before. It was a fine, thick stick. Round it was a broad silver band. 'To James Mortimer, M. R. C. P.★ from his friends of the C. C. H.' was written on it, with the date '1884'. It was just the kind of stick that an old-fashioned doctor often carried.

'Well, Watson, what do you think of it? There is its owner, who is ringing the doorbell. Now is the moment of fate, Watson, when you hear on the stairs a step which is walking into your life, whether for good or for evil. What does Dr James Mortimer ask from Sherlock Holmes? Come in!'

The appearance of our visitor surprised me. He was a very tall, thin man, with a long nose like a beak. It stuck out between two sharp, grey eyes, which shone brightly from behind a pair of glasses. Although he was still young, his back was already bent, and he walked with his head pushed forward in a weak-sighted but friendly manner. As he entered, he saw the stick in Holmes's hand.

'I am so very glad,' he said. 'I was not sure whether I had left it here. I would not want to lose that stick.'

'A present, I see,' said Holmes.

'Yes, sir.'

'From Charing Cross Hospital!'

★M. R. C. P.: Member of the Royal College of Physicians; these letters after a person's name show that he or she is a medical doctor

'From one or two of my friends there on the occasion of my marriage. You interest me very much, Mr Holmes. I had hardly expected such a narrow head, nor such great development of the bone. Would you have any objection to my feeling it? I confess that I am very interested in the shape of your head.'

'I suppose, sir, that it was not only to examine my head that you did me the honour to pay me a call here last night, and again today?'

'No, sir, although I am happy to have had the opportunity to do that as well. I came to you, Mr Holmes, because I recognize that I am not myself a very worldly man, and because I have suddenly met a most serious problem . . .'

Chapter 2   The Baskerville Story

'I have in my pocket some papers,' said Dr James Mortimer. 'They were given into my care by Sir Charles Baskerville, whose sudden death three months ago caused so much excitement in Devonshire. He took these papers very seriously, and his mind was prepared for just such a death as, in the end, he suffered.'

Holmes stretched out his hand to take them. I looked over his shoulder at the yellow paper and the writing, faint now with age. At the top was written: 'Baskerville Hall', and under that, in large, untidy figures: '1742'.

'It appears to be a statement of some sort.'

'Yes, it is an account of an event which is well known in the Baskerville family. With your permission, I will read it to you.'

Dr Mortimer turned the papers towards the light, and read the following strange old story:

'"There have been many statements about the origin of the Hound of the Baskervilles. But as I can follow my family line directly back to Sir Hugo Baskerville, and as I was told the story

by my father, who was also told it by his father, I ...
account fully believing that things happened just as I sh...
describe them. Learn from this story not to fear the results of the
past, but to be careful in the future, so that our family – which
has suffered so badly in the past – may not suffer again.

' "Know then that about 1650 Baskerville Hall was owned by
Hugo Baskerville. He was a wild and cruel man. It happened that
he fell in love with the daughter of a poor man who owned some
land near the Hall. But the young girl always avoided him,
because she feared his evil name. So when her father and brothers
were away from home, this Hugo, with five or six of his bad and
lazy friends, went secretly to the farm where she lived and
carried off the girl. When they brought her to the Hall, she was
locked in an upstairs room, while Hugo and his friends sat down
below and started drinking, as was their custom. The poor girl
upstairs was nearly driven mad with fear by the singing and
shouting and swearing which came up to her from below. And in
her fear she did something that might have frightened the bravest
and most active man; with the help of the thick climbing plant
which covered (and still covers) the wall, she climbed from near
the roof down to the ground, and ran towards her home, which
was three miles away across the moor.

' "Some time later Hugo found that the cage was empty and
the bird had escaped. Then he became like a human devil. He ran
down the stairs into the dining hall, jumped onto the great table,
scattering the cups and dishes, and shouted to all his drunken
friends that he would give up his body and soul to the Powers of
Evil that same night if he could catch the girl. He ran from the
house, calling to his servants to get his horse ready, and to let out
the hounds. He gave the hounds a piece of cloth from the girl's
torn clothing so that they could find and follow her smell. Then
he rode after them at full speed over the moor in the moonlight.
For some time the drinkers stood still. But then their dull brains

to happen on the moor. Everything was
...f them calling for their guns, some for their
...for more wine. But at last all of them, thirteen
...and their horses and rode off after Hugo and the

...y had gone a mile or two when they passed one of the
m.. .ho keep watch over the sheep at night on the moor. They
called to him to ask if he had seen the hounds. The man was
almost mad with fear and could hardly speak. But at last he said
that he had seen the unfortunate girl, with the hounds on her
track. 'But I saw more than that,' he said, 'for Hugo Baskerville
passed me on his black horse, and behind him was a hound of the
devil such as I hope God will never allow to run after me.'

'"The noisy horsemen swore at the man, and rode on. But
soon they became cold with fear. They heard the sound of a
horse coming rapidly back towards them across the moor. Then
Hugo's black horse ran past them, without its rider. After that, the
men rode close together, because they were afraid. At last they
came up to the hounds. These, though they were known to be
brave hunting dogs, had stopped in a group beside a hollow, and
were clearly very much afraid. Three of the men, who were the
bravest or who had drunk the most wine, rode forward. The
moon was shining brightly. In the centre of the hollow the poor
girl lay where she had fallen. She had died of tiredness and fear.
But these evil men were not frightened by the sight of her body,
nor by the sight of Hugo Baskerville's body lying near her, but by
a terrible thing standing over Hugo and biting at his throat – a
great, black animal, shaped like a hound, but larger than any
hound that man's eye has ever seen. As they looked, the thing tore
the throat out of Hugo Baskerville. Then it turned its flaming
eyes and bloody jaws towards them. The three cried out in fear
and rode for their lives across the moor.

'"That is the story, my sons, of the coming of the hound

4

which has troubled the family ever since. Since then, many of our family have been unhappy in their deaths, which have been sudden, violent, and mysterious. I urge you to trust in God, and warn you never to cross the moor during the hours of darkness, when the Powers of Evil are at their strongest." '

When Dr Mortimer had finished reading this strange story, he looked across at Mr Sherlock Holmes.

'Now, Mr Holmes, I will read you something more recent. This is a newspaper, the Devon County News for June 14th of this year. It gives a short account of the death of Sir Charles Baskerville, which happened a few days before that date.'

My friend leaned forward then, and his expression became eager. Our visitor began again:

' "The recent sudden death of Sir Charles Baskerville has caused sadness in the area. Though Sir Charles had lived at Baskerville Hall for a fairly short time, his friendly and generous nature had won him the respect of all who had any dealings with him. Sir Charles, as is well known, made a great deal of money in business in South Africa. He had no children, and he openly expressed his desire that the whole area should profit from his good fortune. His generous gifts to good causes have often been recorded in this newspaper.

' "The events connected with the death of Sir Charles were not fully explained at the inquiry, but at least enough has been done to end some of the stories told locally. Death was from natural causes.

' "Sir Charles lived simply; a husband and wife, Mr and Mrs Barrymore, were his only servants. Their statements show that Sir Charles's health had been bad for some time, probably because he was suffering from heart disease, which caused frequent changes of colour and difficulty in breathing. Dr James Mortimer, his doctor and friend, agreed.

' "Sir Charles Baskerville had the habit of walking every night before he went to bed down the famous Yew Avenue of Baskerville Hall. On June 4th Sir Charles had said that he intended to go to London the next day. That night he went for his usual short walk, during which he was in the habit of smoking a cigar. He never returned. At midnight Barrymore found the front door still open, and became worried. He took a light and went in search of his master.

'"The day had been wet, and Sir Charles's footprints were easily followed down the Yew Avenue. Halfway down the Avenue there is a gate which leads out onto the moor. There were signs that Sir Charles had stood there for some time. He then went on down the Avenue, and his dead body was found at the far end of it. One thing that has not been explained is Barrymore's statement that his master's footprints changed after he passed the gate, and that he appeared after that to be walking on his toes. There were no signs of violence on Sir Charles's body. The doctor said that there was a terribly twisted expression on the face – so ugly that Dr Mortimer did not at first recognize his friend. But this is not unusual in cases of death from heart failure. The result of the inquiry has put an end to foolish stories which have been whispered in the neighbourhood about the affair, stories which might have made it difficult to find anyone to live at the Hall. It is important that a member of the family should settle there and carry on Sir Charles's good work. We understand that the nearest relative is Mr Henry Baskerville, the son of Sir Charles Baskerville's younger brother. This young man was last known to be in America, and inquiries are being made with the object of finding him and informing him of his good fortune."

'Those are the public facts, Mr Holmes, in connection with the death of Sir Charles Baskerville.'

'You say that this article contains all the public facts. Please let me have the private ones.'

'I shall tell you now what I have not told anyone before. Very few people live on the moor, so that one has no great choice of company. For this reason I saw a good deal of Sir Charles Baskerville. With the exception of Mr Stapleton, the naturalist, there are no other men of education within many miles. We became friends through our common interest in science. We have spent many pleasant evenings together discussing the physical features of different African tribes.

'Within the last few months it became clear to me that Sir Charles was a very worried man. He took the story which I have read to you very seriously, and though he would walk in his own grounds nothing would persuade him to go out on the moor at night. He was quite certain that a terrible fate hung over his family. The idea of some evil spirit was always with him. I advised Sir Charles to make a visit to London. I knew that his heart was weak, and the continual state of excitement in which he lived was having a serious effect on his health. I thought that after a few months among the pleasures of London he would come back a new man. Mr Stapleton, who was a friend of us both, held the same opinion. Then at the last moment came this terrible event.

'On the night of Sir Charles's death his servant Barrymore sent a message to me, and I was able to reach Baskerville Hall within an hour. I followed the footprints down the Yew Avenue. I saw the gate where it seems he waited. I noticed that there were no other footprints except Barrymore's on the path. Then I carefully examined the body, which had not been touched until my arrival. Sir Charles lay with his face down. His arms were stretched out, his fingers had torn at the ground, and his face was so twisted that I could hardly recognize him. But Barrymore made one false statement at the inquiry. He said that there were no marks on the ground round the body. He did not see any. But I did – a little distance away, but fresh and clear.'

'Footprints?'

'Footprints.'

'A man's or a woman's?'

Dr Mortimer looked strangely at us for a minute, and his voice sank almost to a whisper as he answered:

'Mr Holmes, they were the footprints of a gigantic hound!'

Chapter 3   The Death of Sir Charles

The doctor's shaking voice showed that he was deeply moved by what he had told us. Holmes leaned forward in excitement, and his eyes shone as they did when he was greatly interested.

'Why did nobody else see them?'

'The marks were about 20 yards from the body, and nobody gave them a thought. It was only because I knew this story . . .'

'What was the weather like?'

'Wet and cold.'

'What is the avenue like?'

'There is a line of old yew trees on each side, which are planted very close together. The path in the middle is about 8 feet across.'

'And there is a gate?'

'Yes, the small gate which leads onto the moor.'

'Is there any other opening?'

'No.'

'So that to reach the Yew Avenue, one either has to come down it from the house or else to enter it by the gate from the moor?'

'There is a way through the summerhouse at the end.'

'Had Sir Charles reached this?'

'No; he lay about 50 yards from it.'

'Now, tell me, Dr Mortimer – and this is important – what marks did you see by the gate?'

'None. Except that Sir Charles had clearly stood there for five to ten minutes.'

'How do you know that?'

'Because ash had dropped from his cigar.'

'Excellent! Were there no footprints?'

'They were very confused. Sir Charles had left his own marks all over that part of the path. I could see no others.'

Sherlock Holmes struck his hand against his knee impatiently.

'Why was I not there!' he cried. 'It is a case of great interest, and it demanded scientific treatment. Oh, Dr Mortimer, why did you not call on me before?'

'There are some matters in which the cleverest and most experienced scientist is helpless. Since the death, Mr Holmes, several strange things have reached my ears. I have learnt that before this terrible event a number of people had seen a deathly creature on the moor like the one in the Baskerville curse. It could not possibly be any animal known to science. They all agreed that it was a gigantic and terrible creature, which breathed fire. I have questioned these people. They are all sensible men. They all tell the same thing about this unnatural being, which was exactly like the hound of the story. There is fear in the whole area. Only a brave man would now cross the moor at night.'

'And do you, as a trained man of science, believe that this thing is not natural?'

'The original hound was natural enough to tear a man's throat out, but it was devilish as well.'

'I see that you quite believe the story. But if you hold this view, why have you come to ask my help at all?'

'Sir Henry Baskerville will arrive in London' – Dr Mortimer looked at his watch – 'in exactly one hour and a quarter. We inquired for this young gentleman, and found that he had been working in Canada.'

'Nobody else has a claim, I suppose?'

'No. The only other relative about whom we have any information was Rodger Baskerville, the youngest of three brothers of whom Sir Charles was the oldest. The second brother, who died young, was the father of this young man Henry.

'The third, Rodger, was the black sheep of the family. He had all the qualities of the old Baskervilles, and they tell me that he looked exactly like the family picture of old Hugo. This Rodger had to run away from England, and he escaped to Central America. He died there of yellow fever in 1876. So Henry is the last of the Baskerville family. I am to meet him at Waterloo Station. Now, Mr Holmes, what would you advise me to do with him?'

'Why should he not go to his family home? To put it in plain words, is there some Evil Power which makes Dartmoor unsafe for a Baskerville? Is that your opinion?'

'Well, it seems possible.'

'But surely if your idea of some evil influence is correct, it could harm the young man as easily in London as on Dartmoor. One cannot imagine a devil which has only local powers. I advise you to take a cab, and to drive to Waterloo Station to meet Sir Henry Baskerville. Tell him nothing until I have decided what to do. Will you return at ten o'clock tomorrow, and bring Sir Henry Baskerville with you?'

'I will do so, Mr Holmes.' He hurried off.

Holmes returned to his chair, looking quietly pleased.

'Are you going out, Watson? As you pass Bradley's shop, will you ask him to send me a pound of the strongest tobacco?'

I knew that it was necessary for my friend to be alone during hours of hard thought, so I spent the day at my club and did not return to Baker Street until the evening. At first I thought that a fire had broken out, because the room was filled with smoke. But it was the smoke of strong tobacco that seized me by the throat and started me coughing.

'Open the window, then, Watson. You have been at your club all day, I see.'

'Certainly, but how– ?'

He laughed at my surprised expression.

'A gentleman goes out on a rainy and muddy day. He returns in the evening with his hat and his boots still clean and shining. He has therefore remained in one place all day. Is it not clear?'

'Well, yes, it is fairly clear.'

'The world is full of clear things which nobody notices. After you left, I sent for a large-scale map of this part of the moor. That is Baskerville Hall in the middle. This small group of buildings here is the village of Grimpen, where Dr Mortimer lives. Within five miles of the Hall there are, as you see, very few houses. A house is shown here which may be the home of the naturalist, Stapleton. Here are two small farms. Then 14 miles away is the great prison at Princetown. All around is the empty moor.'

'It must be a wild place.'

'Yes. It is the perfect place if the devil did desire to involve itself in the affairs of men. Of course, if Dr Mortimer is right, and we are dealing with forces outside the ordinary laws of nature, that is the end of our inquiry. But we must examine all other possible explanations. Have you been considering the case? That change in the footprints, for example. What do you think about that?'

'Barrymore said that the man had walked on his toes down that part of the Yew Avenue.'

'Why should a man walk on his toes down the Avenue? He was running, Watson – running desperately, running for his life, running until he burst his heart and fell dead on his face.'

'Running from what?'

'That is our problem. There are signs that the man was mad with fear before he began to run.'

'How can you say that?'

'I am supposing that the cause of his fears came to him across the moor. If that were so, only a man who was out of his mind would have run away from the house instead of towards it. He ran in the direction where help was least likely to be. Who was he waiting for that night? Why was he waiting for him in the Yew Avenue rather than in his own house? The man was old, and he was not well. The night was wet and cold. Is it natural that he should stand for five or ten minutes, as Doctor Mortimer calculated from the cigar ash that he dropped?'

'But he went for a walk every evening.'

'I do not think that it is likely that he waited by the gate to the moor every evening. Actually, we are told that he avoided the moor. That night, he waited there. It was the night before he intended to leave for London. I begin to see the shape of events, Watson! May I ask you to hand me my violin? We will delay all further thought on this business until we have had the advantage of meeting Dr Mortimer and Sir Henry Baskerville tomorrow morning.'

Chapter 4   The Letter to Sir Henry

Our breakfast table was cleared early, and Holmes waited in his dressing gown for his visitors. Dr Mortimer was followed by a small, eager, dark-eyed man. He was about thirty years old, and was very strongly built. He had thick black hair, and was sunburnt, like one who has spent most of his time in the open air. He was wearing a reddish-brown suit.

'This is Sir Henry Baskerville,' said Dr Mortimer.

'Yes,' he said, 'and the strange thing is, Mr Holmes, that even if my friend had not suggested coming round to see you this morning, I should have come. I know that you think out little mysteries, and I've had one that I cannot solve. It is this letter, if you can call it a letter, which reached me this morning.'

He laid an envelope on the table, and we all bent over it. The address, 'Sir Henry Baskerville, Northumberland Hotel', was written roughly in capital letters. The postmark was 'Charing Cross', and the date of posting was the previous evening.

'Who knew that you were going to the Northumberland Hotel?' asked Holmes.

'Nobody could have known. We only decided after I met Dr Mortimer.'

'Really! Somebody seems to be very interested in your movements.' He took out of the envelope a sheet of paper. A single sentence had been formed by sticking printed words on it: 'If you value your life, keep away from the moor.' Only the word 'moor' was written in ink.

'Now,' said Sir Henry Baskerville, 'what on earth is the meaning of that, and who is it who takes so much interest in my affairs?'

'You shall share our knowledge before you leave this room, Sir Henry, I promise you. Have you yesterday's copy of *The Times*, Watson? Give me the inside pages, please, with the leading articles.' He looked quickly through them. 'Ah, yes – an excellent article this, on Free Trade. Allow me to read part of it to you: "You may imagine that your own special trade or your own industry would be encouraged by taxes on foreign goods, but these taxes would in the long run keep away wealth from the country, reduce the value of the goods we bring in from abroad, and lower the general conditions of life in this island." What do you think of that, Watson?' cried Holmes, in great joy, rubbing his hands together with satisfaction.

'I confess that I see no connection.'

'But, my dear Watson, there is such a close connection that one is actually taken out of the other. "You", "your", "life", "value", "keep away", "from the" ... do you not see where these words have been taken from?'

'Great heavens, you are right!' cried Sir Henry.

'Any possible doubt is settled by the fact that "keep away" and "from the" are each cut out in one piece.'

'Really, Mr Holmes, this is beyond anything I could have imagined,' said Dr Mortimer, looking at my friend in surprise. 'How do you do it?'

'I suppose, Doctor, that you could tell the head of a member of one tribe from that of another?'

'Certainly.'

'But how?'

'Because it is my special interest. The differences are clear—'

'But this is my special interest, and the differences are equally clear. There is as much difference to my eyes between the type of *The Times* and the print of a cheap newspaper as there could be between your two tribesmen. A knowledge of printing types is basic to the study of crime.'

'So somebody cut out the message with a pair of scissors, and stuck it onto the paper. But I want to know why the word "moor" has been written by hand.'

'Because he could not find it in print. The other words were all simple, and could be found in any copy of the paper, but "moor" would be less common.'

'Of course! That would explain it. Can you see anything else in this message, Mr Holmes?'

'There are one or two signs. The address, as you see, is written in rough capital letters. But *The Times* is usually read only by well-educated people. Probably, therefore, the letter was made up by an educated man who was pretending to be an uneducated one. You will notice that the words are not stuck in a straight line; some are much higher than others. I think that shows he was in a hurry. Why was he in a hurry, since a letter posted at any time last night would reach Sir Henry before he would leave his hotel this morning? Did the writer fear an interruption – and from whom?'

'Now we are guessing,' said Dr Mortimer.

'No. We examine possible explanations, and choose the most likely. It is a scientific use of the imagination.' He examined carefully the paper on which the words were stuck, holding it very close to his eyes. Then he threw it down.

'I think we have learned as much as we can from this strange letter. Sir Henry, has anything else of interest happened to you since you have been in London? Have you noticed anybody following you or watching you?'

'Why on earth should anybody follow me or watch me?'

'We are coming to that. Have you anything to report?'

'That depends on what you think is worth reporting.'

'I think that anything that is not usual in everyday life is worth reporting.'

Sir Henry smiled. 'I don't know much about British life yet. I have spent nearly all my time in America and Canada. But I hope that to lose one of your boots is not part of everyday life over here.'

'Have you lost one of your boots?'

'My dear sir,' cried Dr Mortimer, 'you will find it when you return to the hotel. Why trouble Mr Holmes with little things of this kind?'

'Well, he asked me for anything unusual.'

'Exactly,' said Holmes, 'even if the matter may seem foolish. Do you say that you have lost one of your boots?'

'Well, I cannot find it. The worst of it is that I only bought the pair last night, and I have never even worn them. I did a good deal of shopping. If I am going to live in the country I must have the right clothes. Among other things, I bought these brown boots, and one has been stolen before I have even had them on my feet!'

'It seems a strangely useless thing to steal. I share Dr Mortimer's belief that the missing brown boot will soon be found.'

'And now, gentlemen,' said Sir Henry, 'it is time that you kept your promise, and gave me a full account of what has been happening.'

With this encouragement our scientific friend, Dr Mortimer, pulled his papers from his pocket, and told his whole story as he had told it to us on the morning before. Sir Henry Baskerville listened with great attention, and with an occasional word of surprise.

'Well,' he said, 'of course I've heard of the hound ever since I was a small child. Everyone in the family knew the story well, but I have never taken it seriously before. But as for my uncle's death . . . And now there is this affair of the letter to me at the hotel.'

'That seems to show that somebody knows more than we do about what goes on on the moor,' said Dr Mortimer. 'But the important point which we have to decide, Sir Henry, is whether you should go to Baskerville Hall.'

'There is no devil and no man that can prevent me going to the home of my own family.' His face turned red as he spoke; it was clear that the hot temper of the Baskervilles still lived in him, the last of the line. 'But I have hardly had time to think over all that you have told me. I am going back to my hotel now. Suppose you and Dr Watson come round later and have lunch with us?'

'You may expect us. Shall I call a cab?'

'Thank you, but I would prefer to walk.'

'Then we shall meet again for lunch. Good morning.'

We heard the footsteps of our visitors going down the stairs, and then the noise of the front door shutting. In a moment Holmes had changed from a dreamer to a man of action.

'Quickly Watson! There is not a moment to lose!' He ran from the room in his dressing gown, and returned in a few seconds in a coat. We hurried together down the stairs and into Baker Street. We could still see Mortimer and Baskerville about two hundred yards ahead of us. Keeping well behind them, we followed them into Oxford Street and so down Regent Street. When our friends stopped to look into a shop window, Holmes did the same. A moment later he gave a little cry of satisfaction, and, following the direction of his eager eyes, I saw that a cab with a passenger inside which had stopped at the side of the street was now moving slowly on again.

'There is our man! Come on! We will have a good look at him.'

At that moment I saw a bushy black beard and a pair of sharp eyes turned towards us through the window of the cab. Then I heard a shout, and the cab went rapidly off down Regent Street. Holmes looked eagerly round for another, but there was no empty one in sight.

'Was there ever such bad luck, and bad management, too! Baskerville must have been followed ever since he reached London. How else could it be known so quickly that he had chosen the Northumberland Hotel? We are dealing with a very clever man, Watson. He used a cab so that he could move slowly behind them, or pass them, without them noticing. And if they too hired a cab he was all ready to follow them. Would you recognize the face of that man in the cab?'

'I would recognize only the black beard.'

'So would I – from which I guess that it was a false one, to hide some of his face. And now, Watson, we will fill in our time by looking at some of the pictures in the shops in Bond Street.'

Chapter 5   The Missing Boots

'Sir Henry Baskerville is expecting you,' said the hotel clerk.

As we came round the top of the stairs we met Sir Henry Baskerville himself. His face was red with anger, and he held an old boot in his hand.

'It seems to me that they are trying to make a fool of me in this hotel,' he cried. 'They'll find that they've chosen the wrong man! By heaven, if one of the servants cannot find my missing boot, there will be trouble. I can laugh at a joke like anybody else, Mr Holmes, but they have gone a bit too far this time!'

'Are you still looking for your boot?'

'Yes sir, and I mean to find it.'

'But surely you said that it was a new brown boot?'

'So it was. And now it is an old black one.'

'What! Do you mean to say—'

'I only possessed three pairs of boots. The new brown, the old black and the pair which I am wearing. Last night they took one of the brown ones, and today they have stolen one of the black ones! I cannot attempt to explain it. It seems the maddest, strangest thing that ever happened to me.'

'The strangest, perhaps,' said Holmes thoughtfully.

'What do you think yourself?'

'Well, I don't pretend to understand it yet. This case of yours is very complicated, Sir Henry. But we hold one or two threads in our hands, and one or other of them may guide us to the truth.'

We had a pleasant lunch, during which little was said of the business which had brought us together. Later, Holmes asked Baskerville what he intended to do.

'To go to Baskerville Hall at the end of the week.'

'I think that that is a wise decision. Did you know, Dr Mortimer, that you were followed this morning from my house?'

'Followed! By whom?'

'Unfortunately I cannot tell you that. Is there among your neighbours on Dartmoor any man with a bushy black beard?'

'No – or, let me see – well, yes. Barrymore, Sir Charles's servant, has a bushy black beard.'

'Ha! Where is Barrymore?'

'He is in charge at the Hall.'

'Who is this Barrymore, then?' said Baskerville.

'His family have been servants at the Hall for many years. He and his wife can be trusted completely.'

'Did Barrymore profit from Sir Charles's death?' asked Holmes.

'He and his wife each received five hundred pounds.'

'Oh! That's interesting! Did anybody else receive anything?'

'Many small amounts were given away. The rest all went to Sir Henry.'

'How much?'

'Seven hundred and forty thousand pounds.'

Holmes raised his eyes wide in surprise. 'I had no idea that such a gigantic sum was involved. A man might take great risks for that! One more question, Dr Mortimer. Suppose that anything happened to our young friend here, who would become owner of the Hall?'

'Sir Charles's younger brother, who died in Central America, was not married. So the Hall would go to a cousin, a priest in the north of England, called James Desmond. He is quite old, and is a man of good life and simple tastes. I remember that when Sir Charles wished to settle some money on him before he died, James Desmond would not accept it. He is a very good and kind old gentleman. We need not suspect him.'

'Well, Sir Henry, when you go down to Dartmoor you must certainly not go alone. Dr Mortimer is a busy man, and his house in Grimpen is miles away from yours. You must take with you a man that you can trust, and who will always be at your side.'

'Could you come yourself, Mr Holmes?'

'I am afraid that that is impossible.'

'Who would you suggest, then?'

'If my friend would agree to go with you, there is no man better to have at your side.'

Before I had time to answer, Baskerville seized my hand and shook it warmly. 'That is really kind of you, Dr Watson!'

The promise of adventure always interests me, so I said, 'I will come with pleasure.'

'Please report very carefully to me,' said Holmes. 'When the moment comes, I will tell you how to act. But the first thing is for you all to catch the 10.30 train from Paddington Station on Saturday morning.'

We had risen to go when Baskerville gave a cry of surprise. Hurrying to a corner of the room, he pulled a brown boot from under a table.

'My missing boot!' he cried.

'That is strange,' Dr Mortimer remarked. 'I searched this room very carefully before lunch.'

'So did I,' said Baskerville. 'I searched the whole of it very carefully. There was certainly no boot in it then.'

Nothing could explain it. Another event had been added to that number of small mysteries which had followed each other in the last two days – the printed letter, the man with the black beard in the cab, the loss of the old black boot, and now the return of the new brown boot.

As we both drove back to Baker Street, Holmes turned to me. 'I tell you, Watson, this time we have an enemy worth fighting. I have been defeated in London. I can only wish you better luck on Dartmoor. But I am not happy about sending you. It is a bad business, Watson, a bad and dangerous business, and the more that I see of it the less I like it. Yes, my dear friend, you may laugh, but I shall be very glad to see you safely back in Baker Street once more.'

Chapter 6   Baskerville Hall

On the Saturday, Sherlock Holmes drove with me to Paddington Station.

'I wish you to report to me as fully as possible anything which may be connected, even if indirectly, with the case. Any details about the death of Sir Charles, or about the people who will actually be near Sir Henry. There are two families in the houses on the moor. There is our friend Dr Mortimer, whom I believe to be completely honest, and there is his wife, whom we know nothing about. There is this naturalist Stapleton, and there is his sister, who is said to be an attractive young lady. You are armed, I suppose? Keep your gun near you night and day, and never be off your guard.'

Our friends were waiting for us at the station.

'Have you found your other boot?'

'No, it has gone for ever.'

'Well! That is very interesting. Now, do not go about alone. And remember one of the sentences in that strange old story that Dr Mortimer read to us: never cross the moor during the hours of darkness, when the Powers of Evil are at their strongest.'

The journey was a rapid and pleasant one. When the train stopped at a small country station, we all got out and a carriage with a pair of horses was waiting for us. Soon we were travelling rapidly down the broad white road. There were rolling fields and green trees beside us, but behind them the long curve of the moor rose, dark against the evening sky. The carriage turned off the main road, and we drove upwards along a track.

'Hello!' cried Dr Mortimer. 'What is this?'

A steep hill, which was part of the edge of the moor, rose in front of us. On the top, as still as if made of stone, was a soldier on horseback. He held his gun ready over his arm. He was watching the road along which we travelled.

Our driver turned in his seat.

'A prisoner has escaped from Princetown, sir. He has been loose for three days now. The prison guards watch every road, but they've not seen him yet. The people around here don't like it at all. You see, he's not an ordinary prisoner. This man would do anything. It is Selden, the Notting Hill murderer.'

I remembered the case well because of the inhuman cruelty of the murderer. He was thought to be mad, because his actions were so terrible. In front of us rose the open space of the moor. A cold wind blew down from it. Somewhere up there, this man was hiding like a wild animal, with his heart full of hatred against the world. As the sky grew darker, even Baskerville became silent, and pulled his coat more closely round him. We had left the pleasant country behind and below us. The road before us grew wilder, climbing over open slopes scattered with great rocks. Now and then we passed a lonely cottage built and roofed with stone. Suddenly we looked down into a hollow, scattered with small trees that had been bent and twisted by the wind. Two high towers rose above the trees. The driver pointed with his whip.

'Baskerville Hall,' he said.

A few minutes later we passed through the gates, and up an avenue, where the wheels ran silently over the fallen leaves, and the branches of the trees met over our heads. Young Baskerville looked around.

'No wonder my uncle felt as if trouble was coming to him in a place like this. It's enough to frighten any man.'

The avenue opened out at last, and in the half-light of the early evening I could see a heavy, dark building. The whole front was covered by a gigantic climbing plant that reached as high as the roof. From the centre block the two towers rose. A dull light shone through some of the windows, and from one of the chimneys rose a black thread of smoke.

'Welcome, Sir Henry! Welcome to Baskerville Hall!'

A tall man had stepped from the shadow of the door. Behind him, a woman stood in the yellow light of the hall. They took in our luggage for us.

'I must drive straight home,' said Dr Mortimer. 'I shall probably find some work waiting for me. Goodbye. Be sure to send for me at any time, night or day, if I can be of service to you.'

The sound of the wheels died away down the avenue, and the front door closed heavily behind us. Barrymore now stood before us, with the quiet manner of a well-trained servant. He was a fine-looking man, tall and pale, with a square-cut black beard.

'Do you wish dinner to be served immediately, sir? You will find hot water in your bedrooms.'

At dinner we talked little, sitting in the long, shadowy dining hall in the little circle of light thrown by the lamp. There were black beams above our heads, and a high ceiling, darkened by smoke. A long line of pictures of earlier members of the Baskerville family looked down on us from the walls; they made us uncomfortable by their silent company. We went up to our bedrooms early, hoping that things would seem more cheerful in the morning.

I was tired, but I could not sleep. Far away, a clock struck out the quarters of the hours, but, other than that, silence lay on the old house. Then suddenly, in the middle of the night, a sound came to my ears. It sounded like a woman crying. It stopped immediately. I sat up in bed and listened. For half an hour I waited, but there was no other sound except that of the clock, and the movement of the leaves on the plant outside the window.

Chapter 7 Grimpen Mire

The fresh beauty of the morning did something to remove from our minds the dark and unhappy effect which had been left on both of us by our first experience of Baskerville Hall. But it chanced that after breakfast I met Mrs Barrymore in the passage with the sun shining directly on her face. She was a large woman with a severe expression. Her eyes were red, and she looked quickly at me through swollen eyelids. It was she, then, who had cried in the night! If so, her husband must know it. Already there was a mystery round that pale-faced, black-bearded man. We had only *his* story about Sir Charles's death. Was it possible that it was, after all, Barrymore that we had seen in the cab in Regent Street? The beard could have been his. Barrymore might have been in London. What then? Was he working for others, or had he some plan of his own? I thought of the strange warning cut out of *The Times*. Was that his work, or the work of someone trying to upset his plans?

I was taking a walk along the edge of the moor towards Grimpen, when suddenly my thoughts were interrupted by the sound of running feet behind me, and by a voice which called my name. I turned. To my surprise, it was a stranger. He was a small man, with fair hair. He had thin lips and a sharp jaw, and was between thirty and forty years of age. He wore a grey suit and a straw hat. A tin box of plants hung over his shoulder, and he carried a green net for catching insects.

'Excuse me, Dr Watson,' he said. 'Here on the moor we are simple people, and we do not wait for formal introductions. You may have heard my name from Mortimer. I am Stapleton, of Merripit House.'

'Your net and box would have told me that,' I said, 'because I knew that Mr Stapleton was a naturalist. But how did you know me?'

'Mortimer pointed you out to me as you passed. As we are on the same road, I thought I would catch you up, and introduce myself. I hope that Sir Henry is none the worse after his journey? Of course, you know the story of the devilish dog which terrorizes the family? It is very strange how the country people around here believe it. Any number of them will swear that they have seen the creature! The story greatly influenced Sir Charles, and I have no doubt that it led to his death. I think that he really did see something of the kind on that last night in the Yew Avenue. I was very fond of the old man, and I know that his heart was weak.'

'How did you know that?'

'My friend Mortimer told me.'

'You think, then, that some dog ran after Sir Charles, and that he died of shock as a result?'

'Have you any better explanation?'

'I have not come to any decision.'

'Has Mr Sherlock Holmes?'

The words took my breath away for a moment, but a look at Stapleton's calm face showed that no surprise was intended.

'It is useless for us to pretend that we do not know you, Dr Watson,' he said. 'If you are here, then it follows that Mr Sherlock Holmes is interested in the matter, and naturally I would like to know what view he may take.'

'I am afraid that I cannot answer that question.'

'You are perfectly right to be careful.' We had come to a place where a narrow grassy path left the road and disappeared across the moor. 'This path leads to Merripit House. Perhaps you will join me for an hour so that I can have the pleasure of introducing you to my sister? It is a wonderful place, the moor. You never get tired of it. You cannot imagine the wonderful secrets which it contains. You notice those bright green places? Over there is the Grimpen Mire. One false step there means death. Only yesterday

I saw one of the wild horses of the moor wander into it. He never came out. The Mire sucked him down. After these autumn rains it is an awful place. But I can find my way into the very heart of it and return alive. By heavens, there is another of those poor horses!'

Something brown was rolling and struggling in a kind of muddy green pool. Then a long neck rose desperately and a terrible cry sounded over the moor.

'He's gone! The Mire has him. They get into the habit of going there in the dry weather, but after the rains the Mire drags them down. It's a terrible place, the great Grimpen Mire.'

'But you say that you can cross it?'

'Yes, there are one or two paths which a very active man can take. I have found them out.'

'But why should you wish to go into such a place?'

'Well, do you see those low hills? They are really islands, cut off on all sides by the Mire. That is where the rare plants and insects are – if you can reach them.'

Just then, a long, low cry swept over the whole moor. It filled the air, yet it was impossible to say where it came from. It rose to a deep roar, and then sank back again into a dull sound that grew fainter until it disappeared completely. Stapleton looked at me with a strange expression on his face.

'What is that?' I asked.

'The country people say that it is the Hound of the Baskervilles. I have heard it once or twice before, but never so loud.'

'You are an educated man. You do not believe such nonsense as that!'

'The Mire makes strange noises sometimes. It is the mud settling, or the water rising, or something.'

'No, no, that was a living voice.'

'Well, perhaps it was. But there are rare birds that make sounds like that. I would not be surprised if what we have heard was the cry of one of those. Anything is possible on the moor.'

'It's the strangest sound I ever heard in my life.'

'Yes, this is a very strange place altogether. Look at the hillside over there. What do you think of those?'

The whole steep slope was covered with grey circles of stone. There were twenty of them, at least.

'What are they? Are they for sheep?'

'No, they are the homes of early men. They settled on the moor. They kept their cattle on these slopes, and they dug for tin here when the metal sword began to replace stone weapons. Yes, you find very strange things on the moor, Dr Watson. Oh, excuse me a moment.'

Some small fly had crossed our path, and in a second Stapleton was chasing it with surprising speed. The creature flew out over the great Mire, but my companion never paused for a moment. He jumped from place to place behind it, with his green net waving in the air. I was standing, watching, fearing that he might lose his foothold in the dangerous Mire, when I heard the sound of steps. I turned round, and found a woman near me on the path.

I did not doubt that this was Miss Stapleton, since there could be few ladies on the moor, and she had been described as a beauty. There could not have been a greater difference between brother and sister, for he had light hair and grey eyes, while she was very dark, with a proud face and dark, eager eyes. This tall, fashionably dressed figure looked a strange sight on a lonely path on the moor. I raised my hat, and was about to speak, when she said:

'Go back! Go straight back to London, immediately!'

I could only look at her in surprise.

'Why should I go back?'

'I cannot explain.' She spoke in a low, anxious voice. 'But for the love of God do what I ask you – go back, and never set foot on the moor again.'

'But I have only just come.'

'Can you not tell when a warning is for your own good? Go back to London! My brother's coming; do not say a word to him about this.'

Stapleton had given up the chase.

'Hello, Beryl. You have introduced yourselves, I can see.'

'Yes, I was telling Sir Henry that it was rather late in the year for him to see the true beauties of the moor.'

'Why, who do you think this is?'

'I imagine that it must be Sir Henry Baskerville.'

'No, no,' I said. 'I am a friend of his. My name is Dr Watson.'

'Oh – then I have made a foolish mistake. But you will come on, will you not, and see Merripit House?'

A short walk brought us to a stone house standing alone. The trees round it were small and twisted, and the whole place looked sad. I asked myself what could have brought this highly educated man and this beautiful woman to live in such a place.

'It is a strange spot to choose, is it not?' he said, as if answering my thought. 'But we manage to keep ourselves fairly happy, do we not, Beryl? I once had a school in the north of England. Fate, though, was against us. A serious illness broke out in the school, and three of the boys died. The school never got back on its feet, and I lost a lot of money. But I find an unlimited field of work here, and my sister is as interested in nature as I am. We have books, we have our studies, and we have interesting neighbours. Dr Mortimer is a most educated man in his own science. Poor Sir Charles was also excellent company. We knew him well, and we miss him more than I can tell.'

I was eager to return to my post. The sadness of the moor, the death of the unfortunate horse, the strange sound connected with the Baskervilles, all worried me. Then there was the warning that Miss Stapleton had delivered with such seriousness. There must be some important reason for it. I refused an invitation to lunch and, with my mind full of dark fears, made my way back to Baskerville Hall.

Chapter 8   Steps in the Night

I will now follow the course of events by copying my own letters to Mr Sherlock Holmes, which lie before me on the table. They will show my feelings of the moment more exactly than I could by depending on my memory.

BASKERVILLE HALL

October 13th

My dear Holmes,

My earlier letters and messages have kept you up to date with all that has happened in this faraway corner of England. But I have said little about the escaped prisoner on the moor. Two weeks have passed since his escape, during which he has not been seen and nothing has been heard of him. Of course, any one of those ruined stone huts would give him a hiding place.

Our friend Sir Henry begins to show interest in his beautiful neighbour. From the first moment, he appeared to be strongly attracted to her. Since then hardly a day has passed without our seeing something of the brother and sister. They are dining here tonight, and there is talk of our going to them next week.

One would imagine that such a marriage would be very welcome to Stapleton, yet I have more than once seen anger on his face when Sir Henry was talking to his sister. By the way, you told me never to allow Sir Henry to go out alone. These orders will become more awkward if a love affair is added to our other difficulties. My popularity will soon suffer!

And now, let me tell you more about the Barrymores.

Sir Henry tells me that he has given Barrymore many of his old clothes, since the new ones which he bought in London have now been delivered. Mrs Barrymore interests me. She is a heavy, solid person. You could hardly imagine anyone calmer. But I have often seen signs of tears on her face. Some deep sorrow fills her heart. Sometimes I ask myself whether she has some guilty memory, and sometimes I suspect that Barrymore is cruel to her. I have always felt that there was something suspicious about that man.

You know that I do not sleep very well, and since I have been on guard in this house my sleep has been lighter than ever. Last night, at about two in the morning, I woke to hear footsteps quietly passing my room. Soon they passed once more on their return journey. I cannot guess what it all means, but there is some secret business going on in this dark house. I have had a talk with Sir Henry, and we have made a plan. I will not write about it now, but it should make my next report interesting.

Chapter 9   The Cry of a Hound

BASKERVILLE HALL
October 15th

My dear Holmes,

After breakfast this morning, Sir Henry put on his hat and prepared to go out. I did the same.

'What, are you coming, Watson?'

'You heard Holmes warn us that you should not walk alone on the moor.'

'My dear Watson,' he said with a pleasant smile, 'Holmes, wise as he is, did not expect some things that have happened since I have been here. Do you understand me? I must go out alone.'

It put me in a most awkward position. Before I had made up my mind, he had picked up his stick and had gone. But I worried about him going alone, so I set off as fast as possible in the direction of Merripit House. Where the moor path branches off, fearing that I had come in the wrong direction after all, I climbed a hill from which I could get a view. Then I saw him immediately, some way off. A lady, who could only be Miss Stapleton, was by his side. I stood among the rocks, confused about what I should do next. Then I suddenly realized that I was not the only witness to their conversation. A touch of green caught my eye. It was Stapleton's net. He was much closer to the pair than I, and he appeared to be moving towards them. At this moment Sir Henry suddenly drew Miss Stapleton to his side. His arm was round her, but it seemed to me that she was turning away from him. Next moment I saw them jump apart, and turn quickly round.

Stapleton was running wildly towards them. He almost danced with excitement in front of the lovers. What the scene meant I could not imagine, but it seemed to me that Stapleton was shouting at Sir Henry, who offered explanations, which became more angry as the other refused to accept them. In the end, Sir Henry left them, and walked slowly back the way that he had come. What all this meant I did not know. So I ran down the hill, and met him. I explained how I had found it impossible to stay behind, and how I had witnessed everything that had happened. I was so open that at last he laughed: 'The whole neighbourhood seems to have watched! Did her brother ever strike you as being mad? What is the matter with me? Is there anything that would prevent me from being a good husband to a woman that I loved?'

'Certainly not.'

'I've only known her for a few weeks, but from the first, I just felt that she was made for me – and she was happy when she was with me, I swear. But he has never let us be alone together. Today for the first time I had my chance. She kept repeating that this was a place of danger, and that she would never be happy until I had left it. I told her that since I had seen her I was in no hurry to leave it. I would go only if she came with me. Then I offered to marry her. Before she could answer, her brother arrived with a face like a madman's, almost white with anger. What was I doing with the lady? How dared I? Did I think that because I had a title I could do what I liked? Then I lost my temper too, and answered him more hotly than I should have, perhaps. It ended by his going off with her, as you saw, leaving me badly confused. Tell me what it means, Watson, and I'll owe you more than I can ever hope to pay.'

I was confused myself. Our friend's fortune, his age, his character and his appearance are all advantages, and I know nothing against him, unless it is this dark fate which hangs over his family. But our guessing was brought to an end by a visit from Stapleton that very afternoon. He came to say that he was sorry for his rudeness in the morning, and it seems that the quarrel is made up, and that as a sign of this we are going to have dinner at Merripit House next Friday.

'I don't say now that he isn't a madman,' said Sir Henry. 'I can't forget the look in his eyes when he ran at me this morning. His sister is everything in his life, he says. They have always been together, and according to his account he has been a very lonely man even with her for company, so that the thought of losing her was terrible to him. He had not understood, he said, that I was becoming fond of her, but when he saw with his own eyes that it was so, it gave him such a shock that for a time he was not responsible for what he said. So there the matter rests.'

◆

And now I pass to another thread in our story. I sat up last night with Sir Henry in his bedroom. The hours passed slowly by. The clock struck one, then two, and we had almost given up in despair, when we heard a step in the passage. It passed. Then we gently opened the door, and set out to follow. We saw a tall, black-bearded figure pass into an empty room. When we looked in, we found him at the window, with a light in his hand, looking out into the darkness with his face pressed against the glass.

'What are you doing here, Barrymore?'

He jumped back from the window, white and trembling. His eyes were full of surprise and fear as he looked from Sir Henry to me. 'Nothing, sir.'

'Come, now! Tell me no lies. What were you doing at that window?'

'He must have been making a signal,' I said. 'Let us see if there is any answer.' I looked out into the night, and moved the light across the window. I saw a pinpoint of yellow light in the blackness, which also moved. 'Look! Now, do you say that that is not a signal? Speak up! What is going on?'

'I will not tell.'

'Then you leave my employment immediately! Your family has lived with mine for over a hundred years under this roof, and now I find you following some evil plan against me.'

'No, no, sir; no, not against you!' Mrs Barrymore, paler and more frightened than her husband, was standing at the door. 'My poor brother is on the moor. We cannot let him die right at our gates! This light is a signal that food is ready for him, and his light out there is to show us where to take it.'

'Then who is your brother?'

'The escaped prisoner, sir — Selden, the murderer. Yes, sir, my name was Selden, and he is my younger brother. When he broke out of prison, sir, he knew that I could not refuse to help him. He dragged himself here one night, tired and hungry, and the guards were hunting him. What could we do? We took him in and fed him. Then you came, sir, and my brother thought that he would be safer on the moor. Every day we hoped that he had gone. But as long as he was there we could not refuse him.'

'Is this true, Barrymore?'

'Yes, Sir Henry. Every word of it.'

'Well, I cannot blame you for supporting your wife. Forget what I have said. We shall talk more about this in the morning.'

When they had gone, we looked out again. In the darkness was the little yellow point of light.

'It cannot be far away, if Barrymore has to carry out the food to him.'

'The murderer is waiting by that light. By heavens, Watson, I am going to catch that man.'

The same thought had crossed my mind. The man was a danger to society, a criminal for whom there was neither pity nor excuse. We would only be doing our duty in putting him back where he could do no harm. As we reached the moor a thin rain began to fall.

'I say, Watson, what would Holmes say to this? How about the hours of darkness, when the Powers of Evil are at their strongest?'

As if in answer to his words, there rose suddenly out of the darkness of the moor that strange cry which I had already heard on the edge of the great Grimpen Mire. It came with the wind – a long, deep sound, which rose to a wild and threatening roar which filled the air, and then died away.

'Good heavens! What's that, Watson?'

'I don't know. It is a sound they have on the moor. I have heard it once before.'

'Watson, it was the cry of a hound!' There was a note in his voice which told of the sudden fear which had seized him. 'What do the country people call that sound?'

I paused, but I could not escape the question.

'They say it is the cry of the Hound of the Baskervilles.'

'Was it not from the direction of Grimpen Mire? Did you not

think yourself that it was the cry of a hound? I am not a child. Speak the truth!'

'Stapleton was with me when I heard it before. He said that it might be the call of some rare bird.'

'No, no – it was a hound. My God, can there be some truth in all these stories? Is it possible that I am really in danger? It was one thing to laugh about it in London, but it is another to stand out here in the darkness on the moor and to hear such a cry as that. I don't think that I am naturally fearful, Watson, but that sound seemed to freeze my blood.'

We went slowly forward through the darkness, with the black hills round us, and the yellow point of light burning steadily in front. At last we could see where it came from. It was stuck in a crack in the rocks, which protected it so that it could only be seen from the direction of Baskerville Hall.

Then we saw him. Over the rocks rose an evil yellow face, almost like an animal's. It was muddy, bearded, surrounded with wild hair; it might have been the face of one of those wild men of ancient times who lived in the stone huts on the hillside. We jumped forward. At the same moment, the criminal swore loudly, and he turned to run. By a lucky chance the moon broke through the clouds. We climbed over the top of the hill, and there he was, running with great speed down the other side. We soon found that we had little hope of catching him. We stopped, breathing heavily, and turned to go home. At this moment a most strange and unexpected thing happened. The moon was low on our right, and a tower of rock stood up against its silver shape. There, Holmes, black against that shining background, was the figure of a man on the rock. I have never in my life seen anything more clearly. It was not the prisoner. This man was far from the place where the criminal had disappeared. Besides, it was a much taller man. In the moment when I turned to catch Sir Henry's arm to point him out, the figure was gone.

I was eager to search the neighbourhood, but Sir Henry wanted no fresh adventures. He was still upset by that mysterious cry, which reminded him of the dark story of his family.

'A prison guard no doubt,' he said. 'The moor has been full of them since that criminal escaped.' His explanation may be right, but I should like some further proof. The moor with its people and its mysteries remains as strange as ever. The best thing of all would be if you would come down to us.

Chapter 10   The Stranger on the Moor

Now I shall trust my memory, helped by notes I made in my diary. I continue, then, from the morning following our adventure on the moor.

October 16th

A dull and rainy day. The house is shut in by clouds. I have a feeling of danger all the time – a danger all the more terrible because I cannot describe it.

Consider recent events. There is the death of the last owner of the Hall. There are the reports about a strange creature on the moor. It is impossible to believe that it really is outside the ordinary laws of nature. A spirit hound, which leaves footmarks and fills the air with its cry! If I have one quality on earth, it is common sense, and nothing will persuade me to believe in such a thing. To do so would be like those country people who are not content with describing it as a devil-dog, but also claim that it has fire in its mouth and eyes. Holmes would not listen to such ideas. But facts are facts, and I have twice heard this crying on the moor. Suppose there really were some gigantic hound loose on it? Where could it lie hidden, where does it get its food, where does it come from, and why has no one seen it by day? The natural explanation offers almost as many difficulties as the other. And what about the stranger that I saw on the rock? The figure was taller than that of Stapleton. We had left Barrymore behind in the house, and I am certain that he could not have followed us. A stranger is still watching us, just as a stranger watched us in London. If I could catch that man, we might be at the end of all our difficulties.

This morning, Barrymore spoke to Sir Henry privately for some time in the library. Then Sir Henry opened the door and asked me to come in.

'Barrymore has something to say.'

'You have been so kind to us, Sir Henry, that I should like to do something for you in return. I know something about poor Sir Charles's death. Perhaps I should have spoken before. But I only found it out after the inquiry. I know why he waited at the gate in the Yew Avenue at that hour. It was to meet a woman.'

'To meet a woman! Sir Charles?'

'Yes, sir.'

'What is her name?'

'I cannot give you her name, sir. But its first letters were L. L.'

'How do you know this, Barrymore?'

'Your uncle had a letter that morning. It was from Coombe Tracey, and it was addressed in a woman's handwriting. I thought no more of it. But some time ago my wife was cleaning out Sir Charles's room, and she found the ashes of a burnt letter in the fireplace. One little piece at the bottom of a page could still be read. It said: "Please, please, as you are a gentleman, burn this letter – but be at the gate by ten o'clock." Beneath this were the letters "L. L." '

'Have you any idea who L. L. is?'

'No more than you have, sir.'

When the servant had left us, Sir Henry turned to me. 'Well, Watson, what do you think of that?'

'If we can track down L. L. it should clear the matter up. I shall let Holmes know about it immediately. I am much mistaken if it does not bring him down from London.'

October 17th

All today the rain has been pouring down. I thought of the escaped prisoner out on the moor. Then I thought of that other one – the face in the cab, the figure against the moon. Was he also out in that rainstorm – the unseen watcher, the man of darkness?

Hardly a day has passed without Dr Mortimer coming to see us.

'By the way, Mortimer,' I said today, 'I suppose there are few people living near here that you do not know. Can you tell of any woman whose names begin with L. L.?'

'Well, there is Laura Lyons – the first letters of her names are L. L. But she lives in Coombe Tracey. She married an artist who came to paint on the moor. But he left her. Her father refused to have anything to do with her because she had married without his permission. So the girl has had a pretty bad time. But her story became known, and several people round here did something to help her earn an honest living. Stapleton did, and Sir Charles did. I gave a little myself. It was to set her up in a typewriting business.'

Mortimer stayed to dinner, and he and Sir Henry played cards afterwards. The servant brought my coffee into the library.

'Well,' I said, 'has that relative of yours left, or is he still hiding out there?'

'I don't know, sir. I have not heard of him since I last left food out for him, three days ago. The food had gone when I next went that way.'

'Then he was certainly there.'

'So you would think, sir, unless it was the other man who took it.'

I sat with my coffee cup halfway to my lips and looked at

Barrymore in surprise.

'Yes, sir. There is another man on the moor; Selden told me of him a week ago. He's hiding too, but he is not an escaped prisoner, so far as I can make out. I don't like it, Dr Watson. Think of that stranger out there, watching and waiting! What is he waiting for? What does it mean? It means no good to anyone of the name of Baskerville.'

'What did Selden say about this stranger? Did he find out what he was doing?'

'At first he thought that he was from the police, but he soon found out that he had some plan of his own.'

'Where did Selden say that he lived?'

'Among the old stone huts where the ancient people used to live.'

When the servant had gone I walked over to the black window, and looked out at the hurrying clouds and the waving branches. It is a wild night outdoors. What must it be like in a ruined stone hut on the moor! What bitter hatred could lead a man to stay in such a place at such a time?

There, in that hut on the moor, must lie the very centre of that problem which has troubled me so deeply. I swear that another day shall not have passed before I have done all that man can do to reach the heart of the mystery.

Chapter 11   Laura Lyons

The piece from my private diary which fills the last few pages has brought my story up to October 18th. The events of the next few days are sharp in my memory.

In Coombe Tracey, I had no difficulty in finding Mrs Lyons's rooms. As I entered, I was simply conscious that I was in the presence of a very pretty woman, and that she was asking me the reason for my visit. I had not quite understood until then how delicate my position was.

'It is about the late Sir Charles Baskerville that I have come here.'

'What can I tell you about him?' she asked. Her fingers played anxiously with the keys of her typewriter.

'Did you ever write to Sir Charles, asking him to meet you?'

Mrs Lyons went red with anger. 'Certainly not!'

'Surely your memory deceives you. I even remember part of your letter. "Please, please, as you are a gentleman, burn this letter – but be at the gate by ten o'clock!"'

'Yes – I did write it,' she cried, pouring out her soul in a rush of words. 'I did write it. Why should I pretend? I have no reason to be ashamed. I believed that if I met him I could gain his help, so I asked him to meet me in the Yew Avenue.'

'But why at such a time?'

'Because I had only just learned that he was going to London the next day and that he might be away for months.'

'What happened when you got there?'

'I never went. Something happened to prevent my going.'

'You admit, then, that you made an appointment with Sir Charles at the very hour and place at which he met his death, but you say that you never kept the appointment.'

'That is the truth.'

'If you have no reason to feel guilty, why did you at first say that you did not write to Sir Charles?'

'Because I feared that it might be misunderstood, and my reputation might suffer.'

'And why were you so anxious that Sir Charles should destroy your letter?'

'My life has been one endless battle against a husband that I hate. The law is on his side, and every day there is the possibility that he may force me to live with him. When I wrote to Sir

Charles, I had learned that I might have my freedom if a certain amount of money could be paid. It meant everything to me – peace of mind, happiness, self-respect – everything. I knew how kind Sir Charles was, and I thought that if he heard the story from my own lips, he would help me.'

'Then why did you not go?'

'Because just after I wrote the letter I received help from someone else.'

'Then why did you not write to Sir Charles and explain that?'

'So I should have done, if I had not read about his death in the paper the next morning.'

The woman's story was reasonable, and all my questions were unable to shake it. She was probably telling the truth – or, at least, part of the truth. Once again I had reached that wall which seemed to be built across every path in my inquiries. I started my journey back, with the feeling that I would never discover the truth of this matter.

I followed the road at first, and then I turned off across the moor. The sun was already sinking when I reached the top of a hill, and the long slopes below me were all golden-green on one side and in grey shadow on the other. Down beneath me I saw a circle of the old stone huts. One hut still had enough roof left to provide shelter from the weather. A pathway among the rocks led to the ruined opening. All was silent. The unknown man might be hiding in there, or he might be moving about on the moor. I trembled with excitement. Then I threw my cigarette to one side, closed my hand round the handle of my gun, and walked quickly up to the entrance. I looked in. The place was empty.

But this was certainly where the man lived. Ashes were piled in a rough fireplace. Empty tins showed that the hut had been occupied for some time. I swore that I would not leave the hut until I knew who this man was. Outside, the sun was sinking low, and the western sky was bright with red and gold. I sat in the darkness of the hut and waited.

Then at last I heard him. From far away came the sharp sound of a boot striking a stone. Then another, and another, coming nearer and nearer. I hid in the darkest corner, holding my gun, determined not to show myself until I had seen something of the stranger. There was a long pause, which showed that he had stopped. Then once more the footsteps came closer. A shadow fell across the opening of the hut.

'It is a beautiful evening, my dear Watson,' said a well-known voice. 'I really think that you will be more comfortable outside than in.'

Chapter 12   Death on the Moor

For a moment I sat breathless, hardly able to believe my ears. Then my senses and my voice came back to me. 'Holmes!' I cried – 'Holmes!'

'Come out,' he said, 'and please be careful with the gun.'

There he sat on a rock outside, his grey eyes full of amusement as they looked at the surprise on my face.

'I never was more glad to see anyone in my life,' I said, as I shook him by the hand.

'Or more surprised, eh? The surprise was not all on your side, I can tell you! I had no idea that you were inside my hiding place, or even that you had found it, until I was within 20 yards of the doorway.'

'It was my footprints, I suppose.'

'No, Watson. I fear that even I could not be sure of recognizing your footprints among all the footprints of the world! If you seriously desire to deceive me, you must change your favourite cigarette; for when I see a cigarette end marked "Bradley, Oxford Street", I know that my friend Watson is in the neighbourhood.

You threw it down, no doubt, at that great moment when you charged into the empty hut! So you actually thought that I was the criminal?'

'I did not know who you were, but I was determined to find out.'

'Excellent, Watson! Perhaps you saw me on the night when you were hunting the criminal, when I was so foolish as to have the moon behind me?'

'So it was you I saw! But I thought you were in Baker Street.'

'That is what I wished you to think. If I had been with Sir Henry and you, my presence would have warned our enemies to be on their guard. As it is, I have been able to move about as I never would have done if I had been living at the Hall.'

'Then my reports have all been wasted!'

Holmes took a pile of papers from his pocket. 'Here are your reports, my friend. They have been very carefully studied. Now tell me the result of your visit to Mrs Laura Lyons – it was not difficult to guess that she was the person that you went to see in Coombe Tracey.'

I told Holmes about my conversation with the lady.

'This is most important,' he said. 'It could be of great help in this difficult affair. You know, perhaps, that a close tie exists between this lady and the man Stapleton? Now, this puts a very powerful weapon into our hands. If I could use it to separate his wife–'

'His wife?'

'I am giving you some information now, in exchange for all that you have given me. The lady whom he calls Miss Stapleton is in reality his wife.'

'Good heavens, Holmes! Are you sure? How could he have allowed Sir Henry to fall in love with her?'

'That could do no harm to anyone except Sir Henry. Stapleton took particular care that Sir Henry did not make love to her as you yourself saw. I repeat that the lady is his wife and not his sister.'

'But why was he so deceitful?'

'Because he saw that she would be very much more useful to him if she was thought to be an unmarried woman.'

All my unspoken suspicions suddenly took shape and centred on the naturalist. In that colourless man, with his straw hat and his net, I seemed to see something terrible – a creature of unlimited patience and cleverness, with a smiling face and a murderous heart. 'But are you sure of this, Holmes? How do you know that the woman is his wife?'

'Because he told you something true about his life when he first met you. I expect that he has often wished he hadn't. There is no one easier to find out about than a schoolmaster. There are detailed records on everyone who has been in the profession. A little inquiry showed me that a school had come to an end and that the man who had owned it – his name was different – had disappeared with his wife. Their descriptions agreed. When I learned that the missing man was a naturalist, I was sure that he was Stapleton.'

'If this woman was in truth his wife, where does Mrs Laura Lyons come in?' I asked.

'That is one of the points on which your own inquiries have thrown a light. I did not know that she was planning a divorce from her husband. In that case, thinking of Stapleton as an unmarried man, she hoped, no doubt, to become his wife.'

'And when she learns the truth?'

'Why, then we may find the lady more helpful to us!'

'One last question, Holmes. What is the meaning of it all?'

Holmes's voice sank as he answered: 'It is murder, Watson – cold-blooded murder. There is only one danger which can threaten us. It is that Stapleton may strike before we are ready to do so. In another day I shall have my case complete, but until then, guard Sir Henry closely. Listen!'

A terrible shout burst out of the silence of the moor. It seemed to turn my blood to ice. Holmes had jumped to his feet. 'Where is it?' Holmes whispered in a trembling voice, and I knew that he, the man of iron, was shaken to the soul.

Again the terrible shout swept through the silent night, louder and nearer. And a new sound joined with it – a deep roar, musical yet threatening, rising and falling like the noise of the sea. 'The hound!' cried Holmes. 'Come, Watson, come! Great heavens, if we are too late.'

We ran quickly over the moor. But now from somewhere on the rough ground ahead there came one last despairing cry. Not another sound broke the silence of the night.

'He has beaten us, Watson. We are too late.'

'No, no, surely not!'

'I was a fool to delay. But, by heavens, if the worst has happened, we will find whoever is responsible and see him punished!'

We ran on through the darkness, falling over rocks, forcing our way through bushes, struggling up hills and rushing down slopes, always in the direction from which those terrible sounds had come. On our left was a steep drop. The slope below was scattered with stones. And on it there was a strange, dark object. As we ran towards it we saw that it was a man lying face downwards on the ground, with his head twisted under him. Holmes laid his hand on him, and held it up again with a cry. The light of the match which he struck shone on his reddened fingers and on the pool of blood which widened slowly from the body – the body of Sir Henry Baskerville!

We both of us recognized that reddish-brown suit. It was the very one which he had worn on the first morning we saw him in Baker Street. We just caught sight of it, and then the match went out.

'The devil! The devil! Oh, I shall never forgive myself for leaving Sir Henry to his fate. By delaying in order to make my case complete, I have thrown away Sir Henry's life. But how could I know – how could I know – that he would risk his life alone on the moor ignoring all my warnings? Both this man and his uncle have been murdered – the one driven to his end in his wild flight to escape from the animal, the other frightened to death by the very sight of it. But now we have to prove the connection between Stapleton and the hound. We cannot even swear that the hound exists, because Sir Henry was killed by his fall onto these rocks. But clever as he is, Stapleton shall be in my power before another day is past.'

I looked again at the twisted body and the sight brought tears to my eyes. 'We must send for help, Holmes. We cannot carry him all the way back to the Hall. Good heavens, are you mad?'

Holmes had cried out and bent over the body. Now he was dancing and laughing and shaking my hand. 'A beard! A beard! The man has a beard! It is not Sir Henry – it is–'

'Why, it is the escaped prisoner!'

With feverish speed we had turned the body over, and that beard covered in blood was pointing up to the cold, clear moon. There could be no doubt; it was the same face which had looked out at me from above the light between the rocks – the face of Selden, the criminal. Then in a moment it was all clear to me. I remembered how Sir Henry had told me that he had given some old clothes to Barrymore. Barrymore had passed them on to help Selden in his escape. Boots, coat, brown suit – they were all Sir Henry's. I told Holmes how the matter stood, my heart full of thankfulness and joy.

'Then that has caused the poor man's death! The hound was put on his track by the smell of some piece of Sir Henry's clothing – probably the boot which was taken from the hotel – and so it ran this man down.'

46

'But why should the hound be loose tonight? Stapleton would not let it go unless he had reason to think that Sir Henry would be there.'

'Hello, Watson, what is this? The man himself! Not a word to show your suspicions!'

A figure was approaching us over the moor, and I saw the dull red light of a cigar. The moon shone on the man, and I could just recognize him as the naturalist. He stopped when he saw us, and then came on again. 'Dr Watson! That's not you, is it? You are the last man that I should have expected to see out on the moor at this time of night. But what's this? Is somebody hurt? Do not tell me that it is our friend Sir Henry?'

He hurried past me, and bent over the dead man. I heard his quick breath, and the cigar fell from his fingers. 'Who – who is this?' he whispered.

'It is Selden, the man who escaped from Princetown.'

Stapleton turned a white face towards us, but by a great effort he hid his surprise and disappointment. He looked quickly from Holmes to me. 'What a terrible business! I heard cries. That was why I came out. I was not happy about Sir Henry.'

'Why about Sir Henry in particular?' I could not help asking.

'Because I had suggested that he should come over to see us. When he did not come, I was surprised, and naturally I feared for his safety when I heard cries on the moor. How do you explain this poor man's death?'

'I have no doubt that fear, cold and hunger have driven him out of his mind. He has rushed about the moor in a desperate state, and in the end he has fallen over the rocks in the darkness and broken his neck.'

'What do you think about it, Mr Sherlock Holmes?'

'You are quick to recognize who I am,' replied Holmes.

'We have been expecting you in the neighbourhood since Dr Watson came down. You are in time to see a violent death.'

'Yes. I have no doubt that my friend's explanation will cover the facts. I will take an unpleasant memory back to London with me tomorrow.'

'Oh, will you go back tomorrow? I hope that your visit has thrown some light on the events which have troubled us here.'

'One cannot always have the success for which one hopes. In an inquiry one needs facts, not stories or guesses. It has not been a satisfactory case.'

My friend spoke in his most unconcerned manner. But Stapleton still looked hard at him. Then he turned to me. 'I would suggest carrying this poor man to my house, but it would frighten my sister so much that I don't think it would be right. I think that we can wait until the morning.'

So Holmes and I started towards Baskerville Hall. Looking back, we saw the black shape of the man who had come to such a terrible end lying on the moonlit slope. Stapleton's figure was moving away over the broad moor.

'How cool the man is!' said Holmes. 'How quickly he hid his surprise when he found that the wrong man had been killed by his plan! I told you in London, Watson, and I tell you now again, that we have never had a more dangerous enemy.'

'Why should we not call the police immediately?'

'My dear Watson, you were born to be a man of action. You always want to do something energetic. We could prove nothing against him. We have no case – only guesses.'

'There is Sir Charles's death.'

'He was found dead, without a mark on him. You and I know that he died of shock, and we also know what frightened him. But how are we going to make a court of law believe it? What signs are there of a hound? Where are the marks of its jaws? Of course, we know that a hound does not bite a dead body, and that Sir Charles was dead before the animal ever caught up with him. But we have to prove all this, and we cannot do it.'

'Well, then, what about tonight?'

'That is not much better. We never saw the hound. We heard it, but we could not prove that it was tracking that man. No, my dear friend, we must recognize the fact that we have no case at present, and that we must run any risk to build one up. I have great hopes of what Mrs Laura Lyons may do for us. But one last word, Watson. Say nothing of the hound to Sir Henry. Let him think that Selden's death happened as you said. If I remember your report correctly, he has promised to have dinner with these people tomorrow night.'

'Yes, and so have I.'

'Then you must excuse yourself. He must go alone.'

Chapter 13   Holmes Arrives at Baskerville Hall

Sir Henry was more pleased than surprised to see Sherlock Holmes, because he had been expecting for some days that recent events would bring him down from London.

'I've been sitting around in the house all day. If I hadn't sworn not to go out alone I might have had a more interesting evening, for I had a message from Stapleton asking me to go over to his house.'

'I have no doubt that you would have had a more interesting evening,' said Holmes dryly.

'But how about the case? Have you made anything out of it?'

'I have—' He stopped suddenly, and looked steadily over my head. The lamp shone on his face; it was so still that it might have been cut from stone. But his eyes were shining. 'Now that is a really fine set of pictures,' he said, as he waved his hand towards the opposite wall. 'They are all of members of your family, I suppose?'

'Every one of them.'

'Who is this seventeenth-century gentleman opposite me?'

'Ah, that is the cause of all the trouble, the terrible Hugo, who started the Hound of the Baskervilles.'

'Really?' said Holmes. 'He seems like a quiet and harmless person. I had imagined him as looking wilder and more evil.'

'There is no doubt about it. The name and the date, 1647, are written on the back of the picture.'

Holmes said little more, but the picture seemed to interest him very much, because his eyes were often fixed on it during supper. Later on, when Sir Henry had gone up to his room, he led me back into the dining hall.

'Do you see anything there?'

I looked at the wide hat with a feather in it, the curling hair, the broad white collar, and the severe face. It was hard, with firm, thin lips and cold eyes.

'Wait!' He stood on a chair, held the light up in his left hand, and curved his right arm round to hide the wide hat and the long curls.

'Good heavens!' I cried in surprise. The face of Stapleton had jumped out of the picture.

'Ha! You see it now. My eyes have been trained to examine faces and not their surroundings. The man is a Baskerville. That is clear. This supplies us with a missing connection. We have got him now, Watson!'

◆

I was up early in the morning, but Holmes was up earlier still, for as I dressed I saw him coming up the avenue.

'Have you been on the moor already?'

'I have sent a report from Grimpen to Princetown about the death of Selden. The next move is to see Sir Henry. Ah, here he is!'

'Good morning, Holmes. You look like a general who is

planning a battle with his chief officer.'

'That is the exact situation. I am giving orders. I understand that you are to have dinner tonight with our friends the Stapletons.'

'I hope that you will come too. I am sure that they would be very glad to see you.'

'I am afraid that Watson and I must go to London.'

'To London? I hoped that you were going to help me through this business. The Hall and the moor are not very pleasant places when one is alone.'

'Sir Henry, I ask you to trust me, and do exactly as I say. You can tell your friends that we should have been happy to come with you, but that urgent business called us to London. Will you remember to give them that message? Watson, will you write a note to Stapleton to tell him that you are sorry that you cannot come to dinner?'

'I would like to come to London with you,' said Sir Henry. 'Why should I stay here alone?'

'Because it is your post of duty. Because you gave me your word that you would do as you were told, and I tell you to stay.'

'All right, then, I will stay.'

'One more thing! I wish you to drive to Merripit House. Send back the carriage, though, and let them know that you intend to walk home.'

'To walk across the moor? But that is the very thing which you have so often warned me not to do.'

'If I had not every confidence in your courage I would not suggest it. But it is extremely important that you should do it.'

'Then I will do it.'

'If you value your life, do not go across the moor in any direction except along the straight path which leads from Merripit House to the Grimpen Road, and which is your natural way home.'

'I will do exactly what you say.'

I was much surprised by this new plan. Holmes had said to Stapleton the night before that his visit would end the next day. But I never thought that he would wish me to go with him. I could not understand how we could both be absent at a moment which he himself said was one of great danger. But I had to obey. Two hours later we were at the station at Coombe Tracey and we had sent the carriage on its return journey.

Holmes inquired at the station office, and was handed a message:

YOUR MESSAGE RECEIVED. ARRIVING FIVE–FORTY. LESTRADE.

'That is in answer to a message I sent this morning. Lestrade is the best of the policemen, I think, and we may need his help. Now, Watson, we cannot employ our time better than by calling on Mrs Laura Lyons.'

His plan was becoming clear. He would use Sir Henry to persuade the Stapletons that we had really gone, but we should return at the time when we were likely to be needed.

Mrs Laura Lyons was in her rooms, and Sherlock Holmes began the conversation with a directness that surprised her.

'I am inquiring into the death of the late Sir Charles Baskerville. You have confessed that you asked Sir Charles to be at the gate in the Yew Avenue at ten o'clock. We know that that was the place and time of his death. You have not admitted what the connection is between those events.'

'There is no connection.'

'That is very strange! I wish to be perfectly honest with you, Mrs Lyons. We regard this as a case of murder, and it may involve not only your friend, Mr Stapleton, but his wife as well.'

The lady jumped up from her chair. 'His wife!' she cried.

'The fact is no longer a secret. The person he calls his sister is really his wife.'

'His wife!' she said again. 'His wife! He is not a married man. Prove it to me. And if you can do so–!' The angry flash of her eyes said more than any words.

'I have come prepared to do so,' said Holmes, drawing several papers from his pocket. 'Here is a photograph of the two of them, taken in York four years ago. On the back is written "Mr and Mrs Vandeleur", but you will have no difficulty in recognizing him – and her also, if you know what she looks like. Here are three written descriptions by honest witnesses of Mr and Mrs Vandeleur, who at that time kept St Oliver's private school. Read them, and see what opinion you form.'

She looked quickly at them, and then said, with the face of a desperate woman: 'Mr Holmes, this man had offered me marriage on condition that I could get a divorce from my husband. He has lied to me. I see now that I was never anything but a tool in his hands. Why should I be true to him, who has never been with me? Why should I try to protect him from the results of his own evil acts? Ask me what you like, I will tell you everything. I swear to you that when I wrote the letter I never dreamed of any harm coming to the old gentleman, who was my kindest friend.'

'I believe you. Did Stapleton suggest sending this letter?'

'Yes. He told me what to write.'

'Did he say that you would receive help from Sir Charles with the money needed for your divorce?'

'Exactly.'

'Then after you had sent the letter, did he persuade you not to keep the appointment?'

'Yes. He told me that it would hurt his pride if any other man gave me money for such a purpose.'

'Did he later make you swear to say nothing about your appointment with Sir Charles?'

'He did. He said that I should certainly be suspected if the facts became known. He frightened me into remaining silent.'

'I think that you have had a fortunate escape. You have had him in your power and he knew it, but you are still alive. Good morning, Mrs Lyons.'

◆

'Our case becomes complete, and difficulty after difficulty is smoothed away,' said Holmes, as we stood waiting at Coombe Tracey for the arrival of the fast train from London. When it came rushing into the station, a small, active man jumped out from a first-class carriage. We all three shook hands.

'We have two hours before we need to think of starting,' said Holmes. 'We might employ them in having dinner. Then, Lestrade, we will clear the London smoke from your lungs with a breath of the pure night air of Dartmoor. Have you never been there? Ah, well, I don't suppose that you will forget your first visit.'

Chapter 14   The Hound in the Mist

One of Sherlock Holmes's faults – if one may call it a fault – was that he rarely explained his full plans to any other person until the moment when they were carried out. As we approached the moor once again, our conversation was limited by the presence of the driver of the hired carriage. I was glad when we finally stopped near to the Hall, and to the scene of action. We got down near the gate of the Yew Avenue. The carriage was sent away and we started to walk to Merripit House.

'It does not seem a very cheerful place,' said Lestrade, looking round him at the dark slopes of the hill, and at the pool of mist which lay over the Grimpen Mire. 'I see the lights of a house ahead of us.'

We moved quietly along the track as if we were going to the house, but Holmes stopped us when we were about 200 yards from it.

'This will do,' he said. 'These rocks make an admirable screen. We will lie in wait here. Get into this hollow, Lestrade. Watson, you have been inside the house. You remember the position of the rooms. Move forward quietly and see what they are doing – but don't let them know that they are being watched!'

I walked softly up the path and bent down behind the low wall. Hiding in its shadow I reached a point where I could look straight through the uncurtained window of the dining room. Only the two men were there, Sir Henry and Stapleton.

'You say, Watson, that the lady is not there?' asked Holmes, when I made my report. 'Where can she be, then, since there is no light in any other room?'

I have said that over the great Grimpen Mire a thick white mist was hanging. It was blowing slowly in our direction. It piled up like a wall on that side of us.

'It's moving towards us, Watson – the one thing on earth which could spoil my plans. Our success, and even his life, may depend on his coming out before the mist is over the path.'

The night was clear and fine above us. The stars shone cold and bright, while the moon washed the whole scene in a soft light. Every minute the white mist that covered more than half the moor was coming nearer and nearer to the house. The garden wall had already disappeared, and only the trees stood out above the mist. Holmes struck his hand angrily on the rock in front of us and stamped his feet in his impatience. 'If he doesn't come out within a quarter of an hour the path will be covered. In half an hour we won't be able to see our hands in front of us.'

'Shall we move further back, to higher ground?'

'Yes, I think it would be wise.'

So as the bank of mist flowed on, we went back before it until we were half a mile from the house.

'We must not go too far,' said Holmes. 'We dare not take the chance of his being caught before he reaches us. Oh – thank heaven, I think I hear him coming.'

The sound of quick steps broke the silence of the moor. Hiding among the rocks, we watched the bank of mist in front of us. The steps grew louder, and through the mist, as if through a curtain, came the man we were waiting for. He looked round him in surprise as he came out into the moonlight. Then he came rapidly along the path, passed close to where we lay, and went on up the long slope behind us. As he walked, he looked continually over either shoulder, like a man who is feeling uncomfortable.

'Here it is!' cried Holmes, raising his gun. 'Look out! It's coming!'

There was a light sound of running feet from somewhere in the heart of the bank of mist. The cloud was within 50 yards of where we lay, and we watched it, not knowing what frightening thing was about to come out of it. I was beside Holmes, and I looked for a moment at his face. It was pale and excited. His eyes were shining brightly in the moonlight. But suddenly he moved forward. Lestrade gave a cry of terror and threw himself on the ground. I jumped to my feet, my gun in my hand, but I was fixed to the spot by the sight of the terrible shape which had appeared from the mist. It was a hound – a gigantic black hound, but such a hound as human eyes had never seen. Fire burst from its open mouth, its eyes burned, its jaws were bright with flames. Nothing in a bad dream could be more frightening than that black shape which broke out of the wall of mist. With great jumps the gigantic creature was past us. Holmes and I both fired together. The creature gave a cry of pain, which showed that one of us at least had hit it. It did not pause, though, but ran on. Far away on the path we saw Sir Henry. His face was white in the moonlight. His hands were raised in terror. He was looking back helplessly at the terrible thing that was hunting him down.

But that cry of pain from the hound had ended our fears. If it could be wounded, it could be killed. In front of us as we flew up the track we heard shout after shout from Sir Henry and the deep roar of the hound. I was in time to see the animal jump on Sir Henry, throw him to the ground and attack his throat. But the next moment Holmes had fired five shots into the creature's side. With a last cry of pain it rolled over on its back. Then it lay still on its side. I bent down, breathing hard, and pressed my gun to that terrible flaming head, but I did not fire again. The gigantic hound was dead.

Sir Henry lay where he had fallen; he was not moving. We tore away his collar, and Holmes breathed a grateful prayer when we saw that there was no sign of a wound and that we had arrived in time. Already our friend's eyelids trembled and he made a weak attempt to move. Then two frightened eyes looked at us. 'My God!' he whispered. 'What was it? What was it, in heaven's name?'

'It's dead, whatever it was,' said Holmes. 'We have finished with the family devil for ever.'

The terrible creature lay stretched before us. It looked strong, powerful and almost as large as a small moorland horse. Even now, in the stillness of death, the jaws seemed to be surrounded with a sort of blue flame, and the cruel eyes were ringed with fire. I placed my hand on its mouth, and as I held them up my own fingers shone in the darkness.

'Phosphorus,' I said.

'Yes, a clever preparation of phosphorus,' said Holmes. 'It has no smell to get in the way of the animal's power of smell. I am so sorry, Sir Henry. I was prepared for a hound, but not for a creature like this. And the mist gave us little time to deal with it.

You are not fit for further adventures tonight. Wait here, and one of us will take you back to the Hall.' We helped him to a rock, where he sat with his head in his hands.

'We are very unlikely to find our man in the house,' Holmes said as we hurried back down the path. 'Those shots must have told him that the game is over. But we will search the house, to make sure.'

The front door was open, so we rushed in. Holmes took a lamp, and we hurried from room to room. We could see no sign of the man. But upstairs, one of the bedroom doors was locked.

'There's somebody in here!' called Lestrade. 'I can hear a movement. Open this door!'

A faint noise came from within. Lestrade kicked the door just above the lock. It flew open. We all three rushed in, with our guns in our hands. We saw a strange sight. In the centre of the room a wooden post supported the roof. To this post a figure was tied with sheets, which wrapped it round so completely that one could not tell whether it was that of a man or a woman. One sheet passed round the throat, and was tied at the back of the post. Another covered the lower part of the face. Above it, two dark eyes, full of grief and shame, looked at us. In a minute we had untied everything, and Mrs Stapleton sank to the floor in front of us. As her head fell forward I saw the red marks of a whip on her neck.

'The devil!' said Holmes. 'Put her in the chair! She has fainted.'

She opened her eyes again. 'Has he escaped?'

'He cannot escape us.'

'No, no – I did not mean my husband. Is Sir Henry safe?'

'Yes.'

'What about the hound?'

'It is dead.'

'Thank God! That cruel man! See how he has treated me.' She put out her arms, and we saw that they were covered with marks of violence. 'But this is nothing — nothing! I could stand it all — cruel treatment, loneliness, a life of deceit, everything — as long as I could still believe that I had his love. But now I know that in this also he has deceived and used me.'

'Tell us, then, where we shall find him.'

'There is an old tin mine on an island in the heart of the Mire. He kept his hound there. That is where he would hide.'

It was clear that to follow him would be useless until the mist lifted. So we left Lestrade in Merripit House, while we took Sir Henry back to Baskerville Hall. He was suffering from the shock of the night's adventures, and before morning he lay in a high fever, under the care of Dr Mortimer. Many months were to pass before he regained the health he had enjoyed before coming to Baskerville Hall.

◆

Now I move rapidly to the end of this strange story. On the morning after the death of the hound the mist lifted. We were guided by Mrs Stapleton to the point where a pathway started across the Mire. Small sticks here and there marked where the path passed through the green-covered mud. We breathed the smell of decay. The trembling Mire shook for several yards around our feet. With any false step we sank into dark mud. It pulled at us as we walked, as if it would suck us down into the depths. Only once we saw a sign that somebody had passed that way before us. A dark thing was lying on some thick grass which kept it up above the mud. Holmes sank to his waist as he stepped from the path to seize it. If Lestrade and I had not been there to drag him out, he could never have reached firm land again. He held an old black boot in the air. 'Meyers, Toronto' was printed on the leather inside.

'It is our friend Sir Henry's missing boot. Stapleton used it to set the hound on his track. He threw it away at this point. We know that he came as far as this in safety, at least.'

There was no chance of finding footprints in the Mire. When we at last reached firmer ground we looked eagerly for them. But we found nothing. That cruel and cold-hearted man is for ever buried in the mud which sucked him in, in the heart of the great Grimpen Mire. There were many signs of him on the island. We found the ruined mine. Beside it were the remains of the miners' houses. In one of these, a chain and a quantity of bones showed where the hound had been kept.

'Well,' said Holmes, 'I do not think that this place contains any more secrets. He could hide his animal, but he could not quieten its voice. And so came those cries which were not pleasant to hear, even in daylight. The mixture in this container is the preparation of phosphorus. It was a clever idea. Who would dare to inquire too closely into the creature if he caught sight of it on the moor? I say again, Watson, we have never yet helped to track down a more dangerous man than he who is lying out there' – and he swept his long arm towards the green and brown Mire, which stretched away towards the distant slopes of the moor.

Chapter 15   The Mystery Is Solved

It was a wet and misty night at the end of November. Holmes and I sat on either side of a bright fire in our sitting room in Baker Street.

'I have had two conversations with Mrs Stapleton,' said Holmes, 'and the case has now been completely cleared up. The family picture did not lie. Stapleton was really a Baskerville. He was a son of that Rodger Baskerville, the younger brother of Sir Charles, who escaped with an evil reputation to Central America. You will remember that he was thought to have died unmarried. But he did marry and his son married a local beauty,

Beryl Garcia. He stole a considerable sum of public money, changed his name to Vandeleur, and came to England. He started a school in Yorkshire, but the school had a bad reputation, and it had to close. The Vandeleurs changed their name to Stapleton, and pretended to be brother and sister, although they were really husband and wife. Stapleton brought the remains of his fortune and his skill as a naturalist to the south of England.

'His first act was to settle near his family home, which he planned to make his own, and his second was to develop a friendship with Sir Charles Baskerville. Stapleton had learned from Dr Mortimer that the old man's heart was weak, and that a shock would kill him. He had also learned that Sir Charles took the story of the hound very seriously. So he thought of a way to kill him without being suspected of murder. He bought the strongest and wildest dog he could find in London. On his insect hunts he had already learned to cross the Mire. So he found a safe hiding place for the creature, and waited. But the old gentleman could not be persuaded to leave his grounds at night. Stapleton had hoped that his wife would help. But she would not. Neither threats nor blows could make her.

'Then Sir Charles asked him to join him in helping the unfortunate Mrs Laura Lyons. Stapleton, who was pretending to be unmarried, agreed. He soon gained influence over her, and promised to marry her when she was divorced. Suddenly he learned that Sir Charles was about to leave the Hall. He must act immediately. He therefore put pressure on Mrs Lyons to write a letter, urging the old man to see her before he left for London. Then he persuaded her not to go. Now he had his chance.

'He brought his hound, painted it with phosphorus, and set it on the old gentleman, who was waiting at the gate for Mrs Lyons. In the dark Yew Avenue that great black creature, with flaming jaws and burning eyes, must have been a terrible sight. Sir Charles ran wildly, and fell dead near the end of the avenue from heart disease and fear. The hound was called off, and was hurried away to the Mire. It would be impossible to make a case against the real murderer. His only helper was one that could never give him away. Both the women were suspicious of Stapleton, but both were under his influence, so he had little to fear from them. Later, Dr Mortimer told him all the details about the arrival of young Sir Henry. Stapleton's first idea was to kill him in London. He did not trust his wife out of his sight after she had refused to help him to trap the old man. So he took her to London. He shut her up in her hotel room; then he put on a false beard and followed Dr Mortimer to Baker Street, to Waterloo Station and to the Northumberland Hotel. His wife dared not warn the man she knew to be in danger. But in the end she cut out words to form a message, and sent it to Sir Henry.

'Stapleton had to have some piece of clothing to set the hound on Sir Henry's track. But the first boot had not been worn, and so was useless. He returned it, and stole another. This anxiety to steal an old boot proved that we were dealing with a living hound, for which something that had been worn must provide the smell of the wearer. The stranger and more meaningless an event seems, the more closely it should be considered. The very point which seems to make a case complicated is often the one which, if scientifically examined, will throw light on it.

'Then we had the visit from our friends the next morning. Stapleton followed them in the cab. When he realized that I had taken on the case in London, he saw that there was no chance for him there. He returned to Dartmoor.

'When I examined the paper on which the printed words were stuck, I held it very close to my eyes. In doing so I noticed a pleasant smell which suggested the presence of a lady. Already my thoughts began to turn towards the Stapletons. So I was certain about the hound, and had guessed at the criminal, even before we went to Dartmoor.

'I had to watch Stapleton. I could not do this if I was with you, because then he would have been on his guard. I had to deceive everybody, therefore, including you. So I came down secretly when I was supposed to be in London. I stayed in Coombe Tracey, and only used the hut on the moor when necessary. Your reports reached me rapidly; they were sent on from Baker Street to Coombe Tracey. They were very helpful to me, especially the piece about the past life of the Stapletons. I only knew who they were. The escaped prisoner and the relations between him and the Barrymores complicated the case. But you cleared this up very effectively.

'By the time that you discovered me on the moor, I had a knowledge of the whole business, but I still did not have a case that could go before a court. Even the attempt on Sir Henry that night, which ended in the death of the unfortunate escaped prisoner, did not help us much. We had to catch Stapleton in the act. Mrs Stapleton tried again and again to warn Sir Henry without giving away her husband. Stapleton seems to have felt jealousy. But he encouraged the friendship so that Sir Henry would frequently come to Merripit House. Sooner or later he would get the opportunity he needed. But his wife had learned something of the death of the prisoner. She suspected her husband of planning another crime, and an angry scene followed. He showed for the first time that in Mrs Lyons she had a competitor for his love. His wife's loyalty immediately turned to bitter hatred, and he saw that she would give him away. So he tied her up, to prevent her warning Sir Henry. No doubt he hoped that when the whole neighbourhood had agreed that Sir Henry's death was simply the fate of his family, she would keep silent about what she knew. I think he was wrong. A woman of Spanish blood does not forgive bad treatment so easily.

'And now, my dear Watson, I think that for one evening we

may turn our attention to pleasanter things. I have booked seats for you at the theatre. Have you heard the De Reszkes sing? No? May I trouble you then to be ready in half an hour, and we can stop at Marcini's restaurant for a little dinner on our way to the theatre?'

ACTIVITIES

Chapters 1–3

Before you read

1 Discuss these questions with another student.

   a What famous murder stories in fiction or real life do you know?

   b What famous detectives do you know? Are they real life or fictional?

   c Which three of these qualities are most important for a successful detective? Why?

     bravery   patience   a sense of humour   physical strength

     a good memory   specialist knowledge

2 Read the Introduction and answer these questions.

   a What does Sherlock Holmes do?

   b Where does the story of *The Hound of the Baskervilles* take place?

   c What do you know about these people?

     Sir Charles Baskerville   Watson   Selden   Stapleton

     Barrymore   Sir Henry Baskerville

3 Look at the Word List at the back of the book. Which are words for:

   a people?

   b things that you can buy in a town centre shop?

   c natural features of the countryside?

   d feelings?

4 Write the missing names in these sentences.

  a .... visits Sherlock Holmes.

  b .... kidnapped a young girl.

  c .... was followed by a large, black hound.

  d .... was friendly and generous.

  e .... found a dead body in Yew Avenue.

  f .... and .... enjoyed discussing science.

  g .... studies nature on the moor.

  h .... smoked a cigar before he died.

  i .... is arriving soon in London.

  j .... died in Central America.

After you read

5 How are these important in the story?

  a some papers from the 1700s

  b a thick climbing plant

  c a hollow in the ground

  d a large dog

  e Sir Charles Baskerville's health

  f South Africa and Canada

6 There are six mistakes in this report on Sir Charles Baskerville's death. Correct them.

Sir Charles lived in Baskerville Hall with his wife and Mr and Mrs Barrymore, his servants. He enjoyed good health but had a reputation in the neighbourhood for meanness. One summer's night, after announcing his intention to travel to London the next day, Sir Charles went for his usual quiet walk over the moor, but never returned. When Dr Mortimer saw the body, he did not recognize his master's face at first because there was blood on it.

7 Discuss these questions with another student.

    a What information does Holmes have about Sir Charles Baskerville's death? Which information do you think is the most useful?

    b What is the connection between Sir Charles's death and the death of Sir Hugo two hundred years earlier?

Chapters 4–6

Before you read

8 Do you think that Henry Baskerville will want to stay in Baskerville Hall when he hears the details about the Baskerville curse and his uncle's death? Would *you* want to live there if you were Henry? Why (not)?

While you read

9 Are these sentences right (✓) or wrong (✗)?

    a Sir Henry receives a short, hand-written letter. .....

    b Holmes knows who sent the letter. .....

    c Sir Henry wants to go to Baskerville Hall. .....

    d Holmes and Watson follow Sir Henry and Dr Mortimer in a cab. .....

    e Sir Henry became rich when his uncle died. .....

    f Both missing boots are returned. .....

    g Watson and Dr Mortimer go to Dartmoor with Sir Henry. .....

    h Soldiers on Dartmoor are looking for a large hound. .....

    i Baskerville Hall is on a hilltop. .....

    j Watson is woken up by an unusual sound. .....

After you read

10 How are these important in the story?

    a an article in *The Times*   **e** a black beard

    b Holmes's specialist knowledge   **f** money

    c handwriting on an envelope   **g** the Notting Hill murderer

    d Sir Henry's boots   **h** sounds at night

11 Discuss these questions with another student. What do you think?

    a Why is Sir Henry being followed?

    b Why is only one boot returned?

    c Why doesn't Holmes go with Watson to Baskerville Hall?

12 Work with another student. Have this conversation between Holmes and Watson.

    Student A: You are Watson. Tell Holmes everything about your first day on Dartmoor from your arrival at a small country station to the sounds you heard during the night.

    Student B: You are Holmes. Ask Watson for any details in his description that you think are missing. Tell him which of his information might be important in the mystery of Sir Charles's death.

Chapters 7–9

Before you read

13 How might these people be important in the next part of the story?

    Seldon   James Desmond   the Barrymores   Stapleton   Holmes

While you read

14 Put the events in the correct order. Number them, 1–9.

    a Sir Henry falls in love.   .....

    b Sir Henry is angry with Barrymore.   .....

    c Watson is mistaken for someone else.   .....

    d A horse drowns in the Mire.   .....

    e Watson is woken by footsteps.   .....

    f Watson meets Stapleton.   .....

    g Watson sees Seldon.   .....

    h Watson first hears a strange sound on the moor.   .....

    i A strange figure appears on a rock.   .....

After you read

15 How do these people feel about each other? Why?

   a Sir Henry and Barrymore   **d** Stapleton and Beryl

   b Sir Henry and Beryl   **e** Sir Henry and Stapleton

   c Mrs Barrymore and Seldon

16 What is the reason for each of these actions?

   a Barrymore holds a light to the window.

   b Sir Henry wants to go out onto the moor alone.

   c Stapleton apologizes to Sir Henry.

   d Watson and Sir Henry do not go to bed.

   e Watson and Sir Henry go out onto the moor at night.

17 Discuss these questions with another student.

   a Has Watson discovered any useful clues that might help solve the mystery of Sir Charles's death? What are they?

   b What do Stapleton and Sir Henry think about the strange sound on the moor? Can you think of any other possible explanations?

   c Do you think Mr and Mrs Barrymore should lose their jobs? Why (not)?

   d Should Sir Henry take Beryl Stapleton's advice and leave the moor? Why (not)?

Chapters 10–12

Before you read

18 Discuss these questions with another student.

   a Who is the 'stranger on the moor'?

   b Chapter 12 is called 'Death on the Moor.' Who do you think dies? Why?

While you read

19 Circle the correct answer.

   a On the night of his death, Sir Charles was expecting to meet

     a man.

     a woman.

     a group of people.

b Watson learns about Laura Lyons from
Dr Mortimer.
Sir Henry.
Barrymore.

c After his conversation with Laura Lyons, Watson feels she has told him
lies.
the truth.
a story he has heard before.

d Laura Lyons is Stapleton's
sister.
wife.
friend.

e Holmes believes that Stapleton was expecting to
have dinner with Sir Henry.
meet Holmes.
find a dead body.

f Seldon was killed by
the hound.
the Mire.
a fall.

After you read

20 How are these important in the story?
   a a burnt letter   **c** old school records
   b an old stone hut   **d** Sir Henry's old clothes

21 Discuss these statements with another student. Do you agree with them? Why (not)?
   a It was a good idea for Holmes to hide in a stone hut.
   b Watson's visit to Laura Lyons is a waste of time.
   c Laura Lyons does not tell Watson the whole truth.
   d The Hound of the Baskervilles does not really exist.
   e Seldon deserved to die.
   f Stapleton is a murderer.
   g Beryl Stapleton is a bad person.
   h Holmes should tell the police about Seldon's death.

22 Work with another student. Have this conversation between Holmes and Sir Henry.

Student A: You are Holmes. Tell Sir Henry about Seldon's death, but be careful not to alarm him. Say nothing about the hound.

Student B: You are Sir Henry. You are afraid when you hear Holmes's story. You are sure that the hound is involved in Seldon's death. Try to make Holmes tell you the whole truth.

Chapters 13–15

Before you read

23 Will these people be happy or sad at the end of the story? Why (not)?

Sir Henry   Stapleton   Beryl Stapleton   Laura Lyons
the Barrymores

While you read

24 Who or what are these sentences about?

a	He is really a Baskerville.	....
b	Holmes asks Sir Henry to send it back from Merripit House.	....
c	Holmes and Watson pretend to do this.	....
d	Laura Lyons did not know about this.	....
e	He arrives from London.	....
f	It moves slowly towards Merripit House.	....
g	The hound shines in the darkness because of this.	....
h	Mrs Stapleton is worried about his safety.	....
i	Holmes finds it in the Mire.	....
j	She had sent the printed message to Sir Henry in London.	....

After you read

25 Look at your answers to question 23. Were you right? Why (not)?

26 How do these help Holmes complete his case against Stapleton?

    a the picture of Hugo Baskerville

    b a photograph taken in York

    c the rocks near Merripit House

    d an old black boot

    e a container for preparing phosphorus

27 Discuss these questions with another student.

    a Would Holmes have been successful in this case without the help of the two women? Why (not)?

    b How would things have been different if Sir Henry had left Merripit House fifteen minutes later?

    c If you had been in Stapleton's position, what would you have done differently? Why?

    d What does Watson think is one of Holmes's main faults (Chapter 14)? Do you agree with him? Why (not)?

Writing

28 Write a newspaper report informing readers about how the case of *The Hound of the Baskervilles* was solved by Sherlock Holmes.

29 Write a letter of thanks from Sir Henry Baskerville to Sherlock Holmes.

30 You are Lestrade. Write in your personal diary about the events and your feelings on the night that the hound attacked Sir Henry.

31 You are Sir Henry. Write about your dinner with Stapleton and the events that followed.

32 Write a police warning about the escaped prisoner, Seldon. Write a detailed description of his appearance and where he might be found. What should people do if they see him?

33 What happens to Sir Henry and Beryl Stapleton at the end of the story? Do they find happiness together? Why (not)? Write their story.

34 'Sherlock Holmes would not have succeeded in this case without Watson.' Do you agree? Why (not)? Use events from this story to support your opinion.

35 Sir Henry wants to leave Baskerville Hall and your job is to sell it for him. Describe the hall and the surrounding countryside. Why would it be the perfect home for someone who wants to get away from city life? Write your advertisement.

36 Imagine that Stapleton did not die and you are his lawyer at his trial. Your argument is that Stapleton was a weak man under the influence of two strong, dangerous, dishonest women – Beryl Stapleton and Laura Lyons. Stapleton was just a harmless, animal-loving naturalist until they persuaded him to commit his terrible crime. Write your speech.

37 You are Sir Henry and you are looking for a new husband-and-wife servant team because Mr and Mrs Barrymore have left their jobs. What qualities are you looking for in your new servants? What will their jobs involve? What will be their duties and working conditions? Why would this be an interesting and rewarding job? Write your advertisement.

WORD LIST

article (n) a piece of writing in a newspaper or magazine

ash (n) the soft grey powder that is left after something has been burned

avenue (n) a wide road with trees on each side

black sheep (n) a person who is considered to be bad or embarrassing by the rest of the family

cab (n) a taxi

carriage (n) a vehicle pulled by horses

cigar (n) a thick roll of dried tobacco leaves, which people smoke

confess (v) to admit that you have done something wrong, illegal or embarrassing

despair (n/v) a feeling of great unhappiness and no hope

divorce (n/v) the legal ending of a marriage

dressing gown (n) a piece of clothing like a long, loose coat that you wear before you get dressed

fate (n) a power that is believed to control what happens in people's lives; the experiences, usually bad or serious, that happen to someone

gigantic (adj) extremely big

grief (n) a feeling of extreme sadness, especially after someone has died

hound (n) a dog used for hunting

influence (n/v) the power to affect the way that someone behaves or thinks

mire (n) an area of soft, wet ground

moor (n) an area of high land covered with rough grass or low bushes

naturalist (n) someone who studies plants and animals

phosphorus (n) a chemical that gives out light when it has contact with oxygen

reputation (n) the opinion that people have of a person, product or company

roar (n) a deep, loud, continuous noise

scatter (v) to spread, throw or drop things over a wide area

straw (n) the long, thin parts of crops like wheat, dried and used for animal feed or for making things

suck (v) to pull someone or something down with a lot of force

suspicion (n) the feeling that someone has done something wrong or that something may be true

tremble (v) to shake because you are worried, afraid or excited

tribe (n) a group of people with the same race, language and customs who live in the same area

urge (v) to strongly advise someone to do something

yew (n) a tree with dark green needle-shaped leaves

Rebecca
Daphne du Maurier

After the death of his beautiful wife, Rebecca, Maxim de Winter goes to Monte Carlo to forget the past. There he marries a quiet young woman and takes her back to Manderley, his lovely country home. But the memory of Rebecca casts a dark shadow on the new marriage. Then the discovery of a sunken boat shatters the new Mrs de Winter's dream of a happy life.

The Talented Mr Ripley
Patricia Highsmith

Tom Ripley goes to Italy. He needs to find Dickie Greenleaf. Dickie's father wants him to go back to America. But Tom likes Italy, and he likes Dickie's money. Tom wants to stay in Italy, and he will do anything to get what he wants. *The Talented Mr Ripley is now an exciting movie with Matt Damon, Gwyneth Paltrow and Jude Law*.

Ripley's Game
Patricia Highsmith

One night, Tom Ripley is insulted by a man at a party. An ordinary person would just be upset by this, but Tom Ripley is not an ordinary person. Months later, when a friend asks him for help with two simple murders, he remembers this night and plans revenge. He starts a game – a very nasty game, in which he plays with the life of a sick and innocent man. But how far will he go?

There are hundreds of Penguin Readers to choose from – world classics, film adaptations, modern-day crime and adventure, short stories, biographies, American classics, non-fiction, plays ...

For a complete list of all Penguin Readers titles, please contact your local Pearson Longman office or visit our website.

www.penguinreaders.com